Exploring Lakeland Fells

2 : Southern Lake District

by
Tom Bowker

Dalesman Books
1985

The Dalesman Publishing Company Ltd.,
Clapham, via Lancaster LA2 8EB
First published 1985
© Tom Bowker, 1985

ISBN: 0 85206 818 2

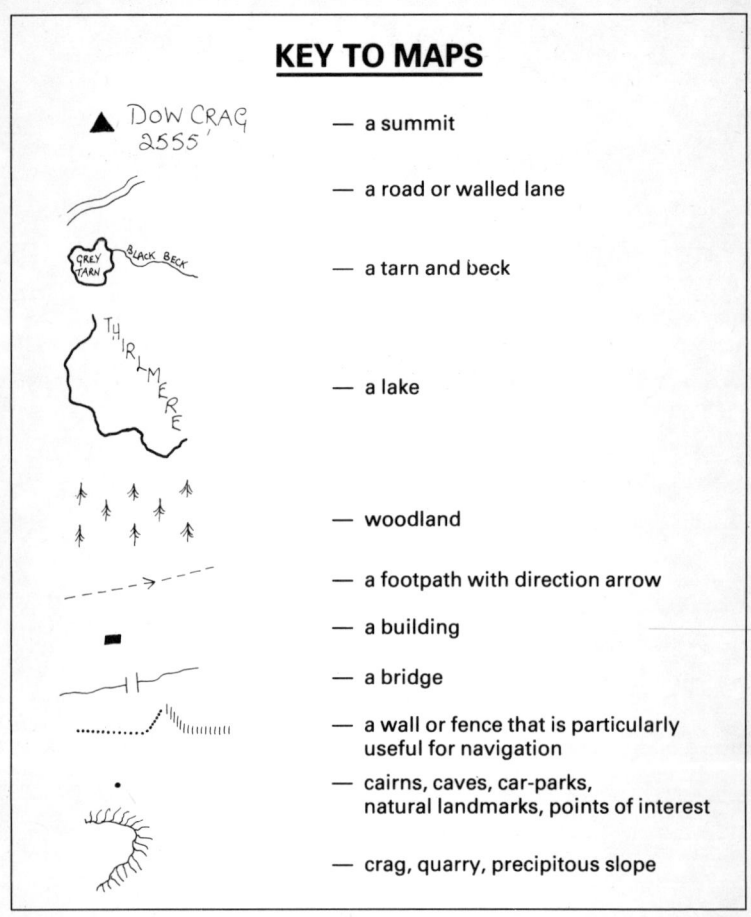

Printed in Great Britain by Fretwell & Brian Ltd.,
Healey Works, Goulbourne Street, Keighley, West Yorkshire

Contents

Introduction		4
Walk 1	Round Longsleddale	6
Walk 2	The Kentmere Horseshoe	8
Walk 3	A Troutbeck Horseshoe	11
Walk 4	The Kirkstone Fells	14
Walk 5	Fairfield via Dovedale	17
Walk 6	Walna Scar, White Maiden and Caw	20
Walk 7	Coniston Old Man and Dow Crag via Raven Tor	22
Walk 8	A Little Langdale Horseshoe	25
Walk 9	Another Little Langdale Horseshoe	28
Walk 10	Harter Fell, Mediobogdum and Dunnerdale	30
Walk 11	The Scafells via the Great Moss	32
Walk 12	Scafell, Scafell Pike and Lingmell	36
Walk 13	The Mosedale Horseshoe	38
Walk 14	Pillar via the High Level Route	40
Walk 15	Glaramara via Cam Crag Ridge	43
Walk 16	Ullscarf, Greenup Edge and High Raise	46
Walk 17	Harrison Stickle via Dungeon Ghyll	48
Walk 18	A Great Langdale Horseshoe	51
Walk 19	Bowfell via Hell Gill and the Climbers' Traverse	54

Cover map by Barbara Yates
Maps in the text by the author

Introduction

FOUR years ago the publishers produced my *Exploring the Lakeland Fells,* which contained twenty mountain walks, plus a variation or two, covering a wide area of Lakeland. This time it has been decided to produce two booklets under the same general title but sub-divided into northern and southern Lakeland by adding more mountain walks to the original choices.

Many are well known 'horseshoes', a self-descriptive type of walk to which the Lakeland fells lend themselves happily. Others are variations on the traditional, or concepts worked out by studying the map or the lie of the land, or on the hearsay of fellow enthusiasts. All are mountain walks in that the primary aim is to reach the top of one or more summits over two thousand feet in height. Accompanying each walk is a sketch-map to be used in conjunction with the text. I do feel, however, that no walker worth his or her salt should be without the one-inch Ordnance Survey Tourist map, or better still the relevant sheet of the 2½ inch Ordnance Survey *The English Lakes* maps. The mileages are approximate and 'left' and 'right' refers to a physical feature as if facing it. A note on car-parking is included with every walk but this situation can be somewhat fluid. Local authorities have a habit of restricting traditional parking sites and/or opening up new ones some distance away from those described. So please don't blame the author if a particular parking situation differs from the text; it is as accurate and up-to-date as I can make it. Those without cars may find problems with one or two of the walks described due to the unfortunate national policy of reducing rural transport.

I feel obliged to say a word about equipment and safety. The style or make of outdoor equipment is largely a matter of personal choice and the size of one's pocket. The range and diversity of it nowadays makes choice difficult and, in my opinion, some of the prices seem exhorbitant. I also feel that price is often in inverse proportion to efficiency. Perhaps this stems from the fact that I started my mountain days in the early fifties when virtually everyone's gear was supplied by the War Department or the Army and Navy Stores and it didn't seem to affect our ability. No amount of expensive gear will get you round a hard walk if you are not fit or determined enough. The walks, as stated, are all mountain walks so, even in summer, certain basic rules apply. Boots are essential and warm clothing, such as wool sweaters, windproof anoraks or jackets, and trousers thick enough to afford protection. Jeans are okay in summer as long as they are loose-fitting, and waterproof/windproof overtrousers are also carried. Knee-length gaiters are an asset, in bog as well as snow. Your pack should contain waterproof/windproof, preferably knee-length, 'cagoule' and the equivalent overtrousers, a survival bag or space blanket, first aid kit, map and compass, pen and paper, whistle and emergency rations such as Kendal Mint Cake. In winter the addition of a balaclava, mittens, torch, spare sweater and socks is advisable, as are thermal underwear and 'long-johns'. From the moment the first snow falls I carry an ice-axe in the hills. Although the occasions when a walker has to bring it into play are rare it helps the confidence by its presence. It is advisable, if you have never used an ice-axe, to practice falling and braking on a slope with a safe run-out. Practice with compass and map is never wasted, it gives confidence for the time when you are forced to navigate by them. One cardinal rule if you are caught out in mist — start using your compass at a point where you *know* where you are, not after you realise you are lost. Then at least you have a point to work from or work back to. If you go alone on the fells take that little extra care, and leave some indication just where you are heading. Mountain walkers, as a rule, tend to be great individualists, but it is only fair to the people who may have to come and look for you to leave some idea of your proposed route. Mountains tend to create their own weather, often bad, and any self-respecting walker should be equipped for it and able to cope. Never be afraid to turn back.

Perhaps that is enough do's and don'ts. The only way to learn is to get out on the fells regularly in all conditions. There will be moments when you are frightened and when you are physically exhausted. Ironically they are the days that live most vividly in the memory and the days when you learn most about the mountains. Don't forget that it is a game, it's enjoyment, it's fun, it's adventure, perhaps the most exciting that most of us will enjoy. There is some danger but the element of risk is one of the basic compulsions for going. For the fellwalker, given reasonable fitness, equipment and the use of common-sense, the dangers are more apparent than real. Statistically you are undoubtedly in more danger in your home or on your way to and from the fells.

The high tops of Lakeland have given me great days of good companionship, physical endeavour and heart-aching beauty. If these booklets help to bring those pleasures to any who buy them I will be well content. Happy walking!

— **Tom Bowker, February 1985**

Walk 1 9 miles

Round Longsleddale

Although one of the most accessible of Lakeland valleys, from the south, Longsleddale retains an air of rugged isolation, especially in winter. The summits rising above its north-eastern flank are largely unfrequented, even in summer. Hereabouts the broad shouldered Pennine takes over from the more starkly sculpted Cumbrian. The summits may be dull but there is much of interest tucked into the rugged flanks and corners of these fells.

Parking: Near Sadgill Bridge, where the 'slate' road begins. (GR 484057).

WALK up the slate road. Buckbarrow Crag rises impressively ahead, and as you approach you will see that it is split into an upper and lower crag. Your objective is the 'climbers' way-down', which zig-zags down the grass and broken rock dividing the crag.

Where the slate road begins to climb past the crag, cross a stile (right) and climb steeply up grass and scree to the foot of an obvious gully, Cleft Ghyll, bounding the left-hand edge of the upper crag. The 'climbers' way-down' starts to the left of the foot of Cleft Ghyll. The right wall of Cleft Ghyll forms a 'classic' rock-climb called Dandle Buttress. From the 'climbers' way-down' this presents itself as a towering, pointed pinnacle — a scene dramatically enhanced if there are climbers on it. The 'way-down' ends at the left edge of the topmost rocks where a grassy groove leads to the crest of the crag. An easterly heading brings you to a fence below a belt of low crag guarding the summit of Tarn Crag. The tall structure peering over the crags is the crumbling remains of a survey tower used in the construction of the Haweswater Reservoir. The insignificant summit cairn lies a few yards beyond.

Now head north to meet a fence which leads you down to the saddle at the head of the lonely valley of Mosedale. Keep your eyes peeled around here for this is red deer country. Follow the fence up the opposite slope to join a wall which is followed to a junction with a fence on the grassy rounded summit of Branstree. The miniscule cairn lies a few yards beyond. From here the energetic peak-bagger may follow the fence north-easterly, for just over a mile, in an out-and-back diversion to 'bag' the summits of Selside Pike and 'Nowtli Hill', passing en route between a fine cairn on Artle Crag and another survey tower. Nowtli Hill is unnamed on the OS maps and requires a short diversion south of the fence to claim its undistinguished summit.

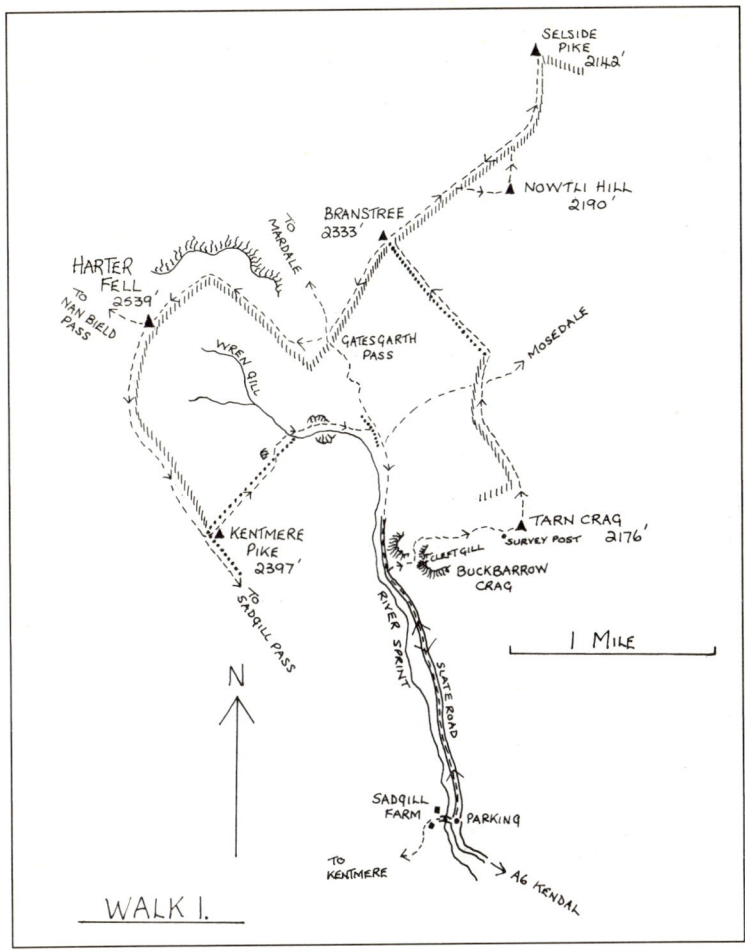

From Branstree, diversion accomplished or not, follow the fence south-westerly down to Gatesgarth Pass. Now climb the well-worn path that cuts a corner to meet the fence again on the south-east ridge of Harter Fell and continues with it to the summit. As you climb there are splendid bird's-eye views over Haweswater Reservoir, marred, I think, in a dry summer by the unnatural 'beach' and the added pathos of lanes and intake walls emerging from the drowned valley. In the boiling summer of '84 the exposed ruins of Mardale brought traffic jams and ice-cream vendors to the valley.

Harter Fell is crowned by cairns incorporating rusty remnants of the old boundary fence, like stands of surrealist weaponry, especially if fronded with ice. From here the rugged eastern flank of High Street is well displayed. Deep Blea Water peeps dourly around a flank of Mardale Ill Bell and shapely Kidsty Pike, balanced on its rocky plinth, rises beyond the serrated Rough Crag/Long Stile ridge.

Now follow the fence south, then south-east, to Kentmere Pike. Just below the summit of this fell the fence is superseded by a wall and the trig point lies beyond it. Close to the trig-point a wall heads north-easterly, down to Wren Gill. Follow this. Shortly before you reach the gill a man-made cave entrance lies over the wall to your left. Cross Wren Gill and follow it down into extensive old quarry workings. Here it spills in a fine cascade into a boulder-choked pit where it is swallowed in some subterranean labyrinth before being regurgitated into daylight some distance away. It appears likely that this quarry is the one referred to in a document of Edward I's reign which contains the earliest recorded reference to a Lakeland quarry. Continue through the quarry to a stile leading onto the slate road. Return down this.

Walk 2   **12 miles**

The Kentmere Horseshoe

Considering that from the south it is the most accessible of Lakeland valleys, Kentmere remains remarkably uncrowded. It does not hide itself. From the Kendal by-pass it displays its wares for all to see. The eye is drawn to the interesting profile of Ill Bell, and beyond it to where the southern ramparts of High Street block the dalehead. They present an irresistible challenge, especially when draped with snow. Perhaps it is because when the A591 drops down towards Staveley, the gateway to Kentmere, the eye is drawn westward to more dramatic skylines.

Parking: In Kentmere village, near the church. (GR 456042).

WALK up the narrowing road to a gate. Turn left here towards some farm buildings. On the corner of one the way to Garburn Pass is clearly indicated. The track, walled at first, climbs steadily up the western flank of the valley. Below the left wall Kentmere Hall, a crumbling 'pele' tower, was once the home of the Gilpins, who named medieval warriors, Elizabethan churchmen and diplomats, and eighteenth-century educationalists amongst their number. Its crenellations are a reminder that when Wallace and Bruce raided, these lovely hills and valleys witnessed bloodshed and atrocity.

The crest of Garburn Pass is crowned by a gate. Turn right and follow the wall northwards for just over a mile to where it turns away. Leave it here and head for the crest beyond, and disappointment when you find the summit of Yoke lies a little further. From the northern end of Yoke summit Ill Bell is gracefully imposing. Below lies Kentmere Reservoir with the notch of Nan Bield Pass and rounded Harter Fell beyond. A dip in the ridge followed by a steep climb captures multiple-cairned Ill Bell followed by a repeat performance to gain the summit of Froswick. Beyond Froswick the ridge dips then rises again. Below, leftwards, the converging line of the Roman military road is clearly visible. The ridge joins the High Street massif near an old iron fence post where paths divide. The path bearing right crosses the head of a gully before tortuously following the valley rim around to Nan Bield. It makes an abbreviated horseshoe if enthusiasm wanes or the weather turns nasty.

If not, take the left-hand path and head north-west to meet a tail of crumbling wall which leads up to the shapely chimney-like cairn crowning Thornthwaite Crag, and a fine view of notched and craggy fells rolling away westwards. The lee of this beautifully constructed cairn and its supporting wall is a good spot for a breather. North-easterly a broad gentle dip leads towards High Street and its crowning wall. The path breaching the wall is the probable line of the Roman road, passing to the west of the High Street trig point. None of the stones that once paved it remain, but doubtless the walls of many an old Lakeland dwelling contain the handiwork of those redoubtable legionaries. From Thornthwaite Crag head for the High Street wall corner and follow the wall up to reach the trig point.

Thirteenth-century cartographers referred to High Street as 'Brettestreete' or the 'street of the Britons', which implies that this broad undulating ridge is one of the ancient highways of England. Well above two thousand feet for most of its length it would be clear of even the highest forest which would mean faster travel and freedom from possible ambush. The Romans would be quick to grasp these advantages. From the trig point head north-east to a

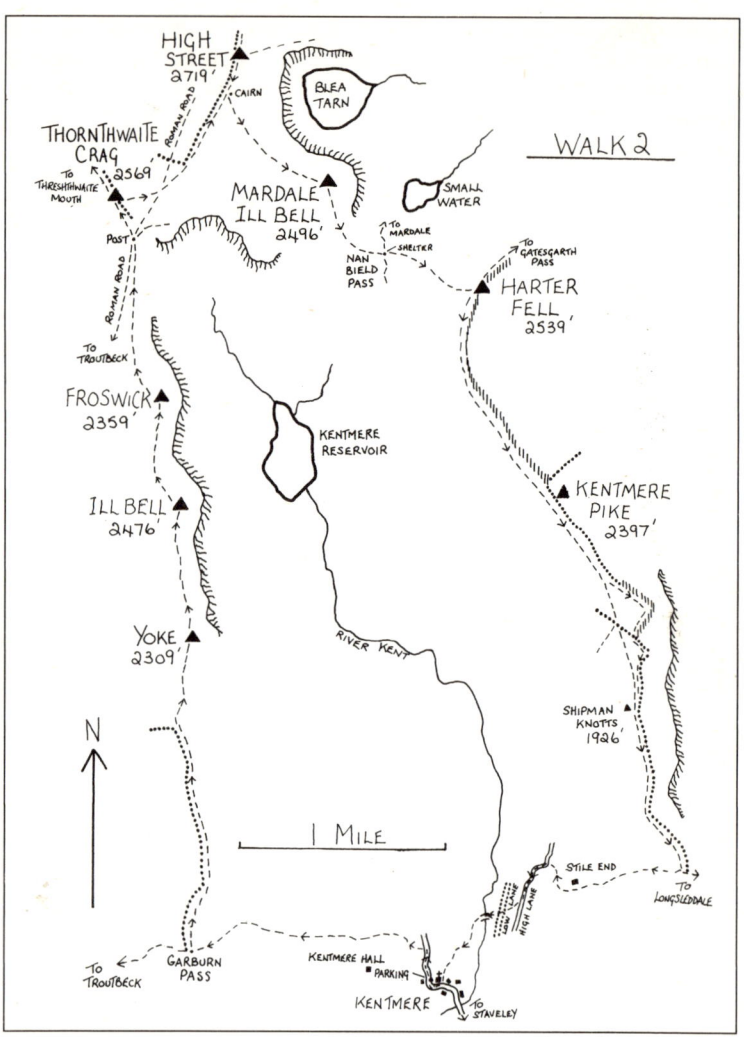

small cairn on the rim of the fell. Here look down on the Long Stile ridge which divides Riggindale, on the left, from gloomy Blea Water, with the gleaming curve of Haweswater beyond.

Return to the trig point and retrace your steps back down the wall to where a cairn marks the beginning of a path heading south-easterly towards Mardale Ill Bell. In bad weather the compass may be needed here for this path is indistinct and the ground falls away precipitously towards Blea Water. Beyond the Mardale Ill Bell cairn the path improves and leads easily down to the narrow windswept notch of Nan Bield Pass and its well constructed windbreak. Down to your right Kentmere Reservoir is overshadowed by a volcano-like Ill Bell, and leftwards the rock-girt gem of Small Water leads the eye delightfully down to Haweswater beyond. Climb up the far flank of the pass, where an entertaining and rocky ridge leads to the surreal cairn crowning Harter Fell's grassy dome.

Now turn right, south, and follow the fence, which is eventually superseded by a wall, along the broad grassy ridge towards Kentmere Pike. This final leg of the walk is rather an anti-climax, the terrain being somewhat dull and monotonous. Beyond Kentmere Pike continue with the wall, or fence, along the ridge crest, ignoring a corner-cutting path to your right, for some interesting views down into the depths of Longsleddale. Continue over Shipman Knotts and eventually down to meet the Sadgill–Kentmere bridle path. Turn right and follow this down, passing a barn, Stile End, to reach a tarmac road. Turn left along this until a stile in the right wall is reached. Cross this and go down to cross a stile leading into a walled lane, Low Lane. Climb the stile in the opposite wall and go down to a footbridge over the River Kent. Cross the field beyond to a lane and follow this leftwards to eventually reach Kentmere church.

Walk 3   **12 miles**

A Troutbeck Horseshoe

I can't recall seeing a Troutbeck Horseshoe listed amongst these traditional Lakeland walks. Perhaps the fact that the busy A592 crossed the natural line of such a walk offends the purists. Nevertheless this lovely valley warrants a horseshoe so here's my offering. It provides varied and interesting walking and splendid views.

Parking: Park on the A592, just north of Troutbeck church, in either of two lay-bys (GR 414029).

WALK across the road and enter the Limefitt Caravan and Camping Site. Follow the road through the site and up towards the farm. Just below it turn left at a multi-armed signpost, pass the ablutions block, then turn right through a gap in a wall onto a stony path leading behind the farm. Turn left around a wall, pass through a metal gate and continue up to join a higher path. Turn left. Now almost immediately look for a path slanting up the steep fellside on your right towards a dark plantation. Climb this to reach a stile leading onto the Garburn Road. Follow this rough, ancient mountain highway up to the gate crowning its crest.

From the Garburn gate head north, on either side of a wall. The way over the fine trio of Yoke, Ill Bell and Froswick is obvious and needs no description. Shapely peak follows shapely peak, the ground falls away steeply on either hand, and the views of lake and fell are widespread and constantly changing. It is Lakeland fell-walking at its best, especially in winter. Beyond Froswick the ridge climbs again. Below, leftwards, the converging line of the Roman military road is clearly visible. The ridge joins the High Street massif near an old iron fence post where paths fork.

Now head north-westerly to meet the crumbling tail of an old wall which leads up to the shapely, chimney-like cairn crowning Thornthwaite Crag, the high point of the horseshoe. North-westerly, down the bowl of Thresthwaite Cove, lie the dark headwaters of Ullswater, whilst to the south Windermere aims its gleaming, island-flecked blade at a distant glint of Morecambe Bay. Into the western arc, from Coniston Old Man to Catstycam, is packed a rugged, crag-flanked and gill-slashed skyline such as to set even tiring feet twitching in anticipation.

Now keep to the western side of a wall which heads north-westerly before swinging west and steeply down to the high grassy saddle of Thresthwaite Mouth. Continue with the wall up the far flank in a steep, interesting and surprisingly rocky scramble. Eventually the angle eases and the path veers away from the wall to reach the summit cairn of John Bell's Banner close to a junction of walls.

From the cairn head west, through a gap in a crossing wall, to follow a wall heading west with a worn path alongside it. This path and wall can be followed all the way to the back door of the Kirkstone Pass Inn. For obvious reasons this is the fell's 'tourist route' and, ironically, like so many popular paths is the most boring and uninteresting way to the summit. Shortly after passing a shallow tarn the wall/path swings south-westerly. Away on the skyline to your right, hereabouts, is a memorial to one Mark Atkinson, a licensee of the Kirkstone Pass Inn for many years. From it there is a fine view of the pass. When the wall reaches the dip below the

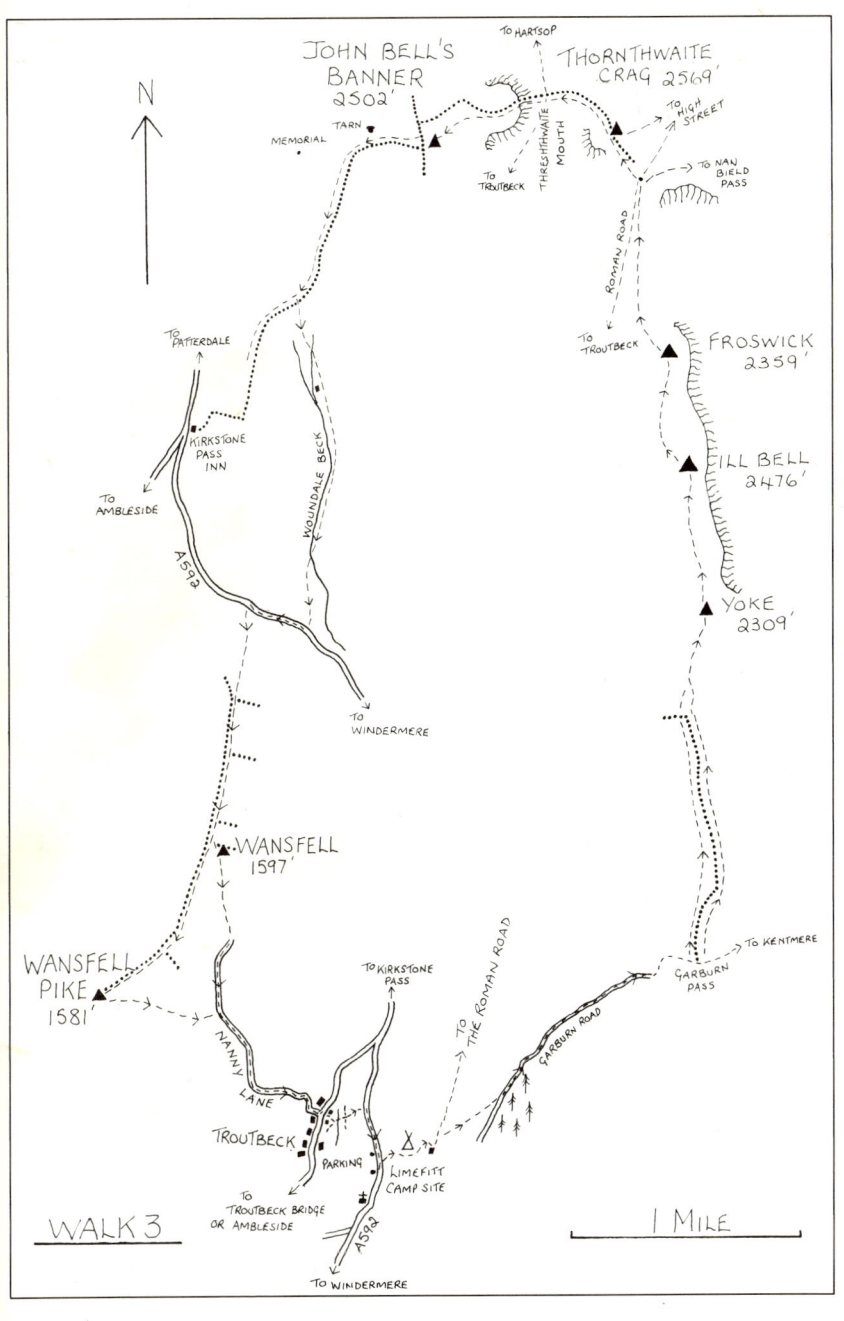

pronounced eminence of St. Raven's Edge go left, through gaps in it, and head down into the high valley of Woundale. Keep to the left bank of Woundale Beck, passing a ruin and some pleasant cascades. Near the ruin a path is met and a mile further on it leads you onto the A592.

Now walk up the road to a gate on your left. Go through the gate and follow a path to a gap in a wall. Wainwright describes this section as an 'uninteresting trudge . . . and awkward walls have to be climbed'. I don't recommend you climb walls, there are gaps and stiles if you look. A mile of this reaches the summit of Wansfell. From here you can head south, to find a stile leading into a walled lane, Nanny Lane, which takes you down to Troutbeck. If you are still feeling energetic, however, continue along the undulating ridge to reach the popular viewpoint of Wansfell Pike. From here a cairned path takes you east to Nanny Lane.

Nanny Lane is not a drove road or ancient highway, rather a kind of funnel built for moving sheep quickly down the fellside. When the tarmac road is reached turn left and almost immediately right down a narrow path between walls. At a T-junction turn left, crossing over a beck, to reach a crossroads. Continue up the tarmac lane ahead to shortly come out on the A592 just north of your car.

Walk 4   **7 miles**

The Kirkstone Fells

From most angles these fells present plebian profiles. Yet this walk offers much of interest — old quarries, possible red deer sightings and a surprising amount of easy scrambling. It is only from near Hartsop Hall Farm, where almost the entire walk can be seen in profile, that one becomes aware that these are three very graceful and steeply sculpted hills.

Parking: By the bridge where the A592 crosses the Caudale Beck, about a quarter of a mile south of the Brotherswater Hotel. (GR 403115).

GO through the metal gate on the south side of the bridge and climb the path running alongside the beck. Soon it turns away from the beck and spirals up a steep grassy ridge. As you climb there is a fine view backwards into Dovedale, dominated by the pale steep rocks of Dove Crag. Rising above the Hartsop-above-How ridge are the rugged profiles of Fairfield and St. Sunday Crag. The spirals you are climbing are the remains of an old 'sledgate' down which quarrymen steered sleds, or 'trailbarrows', loaded with a quarter of a ton of slate, running before their creaking loads like a horse. The old quarry workings lie on the left flank of the ridge overlooking Caudale, a lonely mountain sanctuary which is often the haunt of red deer. I've seen deer too picking their way across the shaly western flank of this ridge, oblivious to the summer traffic choking the Kirkstone zig-zags below them.

As the ridge flattens out into the summit plateau the path becomes indistinct but if the left-hand rim is adhered to a large cairn soon looms ahead. Easterly, beyond a small tarn, stone walls crowd the skyline. Head for these and the summit cairn lies just beyond a wall junction. (See Walk 3 for the derivation of John Bell's Banner). Descend by following the wall and path which heads west, then south-west, climbing over the rocky hump of St. Raven's Edge, to eventually reach the Kirkstone Pass Inn.

Cross the road and attack the craggy south-eastern flank of Red Screes. The route is obvious, a fault line running diagonally through the crags from left to right. Easier alternatives can be found by bearing left into the combe whose sanguine crags and screes give the mountain its name. The tumbled wall straggling up the grassy slopes below the combe was documented in the Troutbeck Painable Fence Book of 1680. Walls had to be maintained on 'pain' of a fine of 6s 8d! This route, taken winter or summer, with exhilarating views of the tiny whitewashed inn and the twisting ribbon of road virtually beneath one's heels, makes Red Screes one of the most excitingly accessible of Lakeland tops.

The trig point stands on the northern rim, overlooking Brotherswater, close to a shallow tarn. In contrast to the rock-shattered face just climbed, the summit is broad and grassy. the view is superb, especially the south-to-north-west arc, from gleaming, island-studded Windermere to high and hoary Helvellyn. Now head westerly down gentle grass slopes to a junction of walls. Follow the north-westerly wall down steepening slopes to the stile crowning the crest of Scandale Pass.

From here the next top, Little Hart Crag, belies its appearance from other angles by showing a craggy twin-peaked profile. To reach it climb up alongside the wall and when this veers left leave it and head towards the foot of the left-hand and highest peak. For those inclined that way a variety of short scrambles can be enjoyed

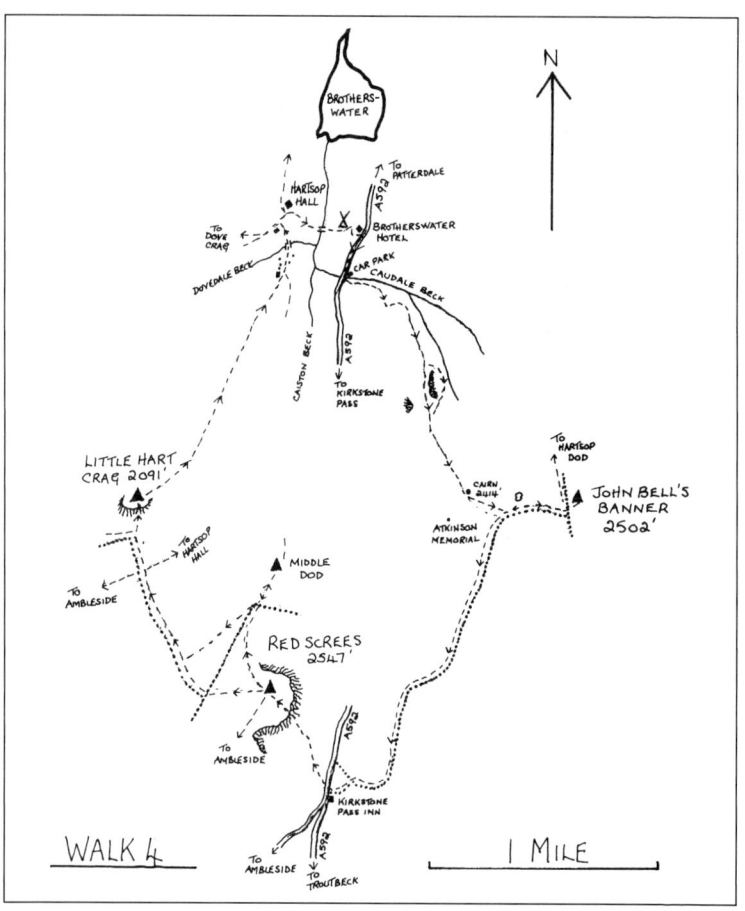

on the flanks of this craggy little fell. From the cairn Dove Crag can be seen in profile, a true guide to its unrelenting steepness.

Descend over the subsidiary top and along a broad gently angled ridge which soon narrows and plunges steeply down into Dovedale. At its base, near a barn, join the path linking Patterdale to Ambleside over Scandale Pass. Turn left and follow it through 'standing stones', across a footbridge and through sheep-pens to emerge on a path near Hartsop Hall Farm. Turn right, towards the farm, then right again to follow the path across fields to the campsite below the Brotherswater Hotel. Here a refreshing drink will set you up for the short walk back up the road to your car.

Walk 5   9 miles

Fairfield via Dovedale

Fairfield is a prosaic name for one of Lakeland's highest mountains, but then from many points of the compass it is a prosaic-looking fell. From the north it is obscured by the bulk of Helvellyn. From the west it is a nondescript lump. From the south, from Ambleside, it certainly commands attention but more because of its bulk than its profile, any grace being provided by its outliers Heron and High Pikes. It is on its north-eastern edges where the true worth of this fell lies. Here the glaciers have sculpted crags, high rugged coves and two lovely valleys, and time has honed them to a rare finish.

Parking: In the car park near Cow Bridge, where the A592 crosses the Goldrill Beck, about a mile and a half south of Patterdale. (GR 403134).

GO through the gate behind the car park and follow the wooded track, along the shore of Brotherswater, to Hartsop Hall Farm. Beyond the last barn the path forks; take the right-hand path signposted 'Dove Crag'. After passing below old mine workings the path is followed through a wood for about a mile. The woods end at a wall. Beyond it the valley ahead can be seen to narrow and curve to the left, the path clinging to its right wall. Immediately above and to your right are the clean rocks of Gill Crag or Dovedale Slabs. A handful of amiable rock-climbs can be enjoyed on these sun-facing slabs. At the head of the valley aptly-named Black Crag acts as a drainage channel for the upper fell and is invariably discoloured by seeping water.

The scene which greets the eye as you follow the path, as it twists and climbs leftwards at the head of the valley, is as wild and magnificent as any in Lakeland. Towering ahead, above a sweep of scree and a tumble of massive weathered boulders, is the stark face of Dove Crag. It has not the massiveness of Scafell Crag, Pavey Ark or Dow, but its line is relentless and many of Britain's finest climbers have been drawn by its immutable challenge.

Shortly after crossing a beck the path veers right and for several hundred feet climbs steeply up to the right of the crag following a grassy groove bounded by thrusting ribs of rock. This steep section ends with a wet rocky corner, which can be avoided. Beyond this, grassy slopes fall back and at this point an interesting diversion can be made. Turn left and cross grass and scree to where an obvious rocky rake leads around onto the face of Dove Crag. This leads up to a broad grassy ledge in front of a surprisingly large cave. A dozen

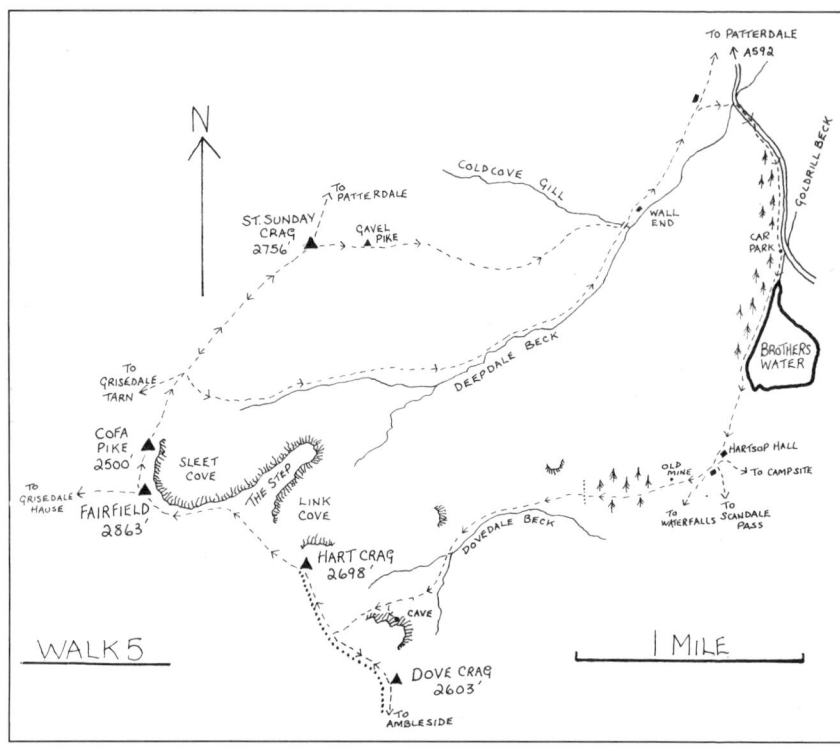

or so people could bivouac quite comfortably here, and do. There is a theory bandied about that it is not a natural cave but a 'priest hole' hacked or blasted out by fellsmen loyal to the Old Faith.

Return to the path and continue with it past a boggy basin. Soon steeper climbing and cairns lead to the wall crowning the saddle between Dove Crag fell and Hart Crag. Turn left and follow the wall for about a third of a mile to 'bag' Dove Crag and an extensive view southwards. Return to the saddle and climb north-westerly to capture the rocky summit of Hart Crag. From here descend to Link Hause, where you can look down into wild Link Cove with the green drumlin-dimpled length of Deepdale beyond. On the left wall of Link Cove, Scrubby Crag provides some of the steepest and hardest climbing in the eastern fells. The path now climbs onto the crest of a broad grassy ridge, the neck of a rocky spur called The Step which, thrusting north-eastwards out of the Fairfield massif, divides upper Deepdale into Link and Sleet Coves. Turning west along this ridge the path climbs gently up to the Fairfield summit plateau. As it approaches, the path swings north-westerly and, nearing the precipitous rim of Sleet Cove, crosses the head of Flinty Grave — an obvious scree-shoot.

Two rough stone windbreaks crown Fairfield, one balanced on the eastern rim, the other more centrally placed. North of the latter a cairn stands on a rocky plinth. Viewed from differing angles each appears to be the summit cairn. The view is extensive. Highlights are the gleaming waters of Windermere, Esthwaite and Coniston to the south; beyond gleams Morecambe Bay. Westerly the thrusting dome of Gable dominates a superb mountain skyline ranging from Coniston Old Man to Grisedale Pike. Helvellyn and its splendid outliers sprawl across the northern sky. The summit of Fairfield is a potentially hazardous place in winter. The north-east rim drops abruptly away over crags and substantial cornices build up quickly there. In a blizzard or white-out the unwary or inexperienced may, and have, found themselves walking into a deathtrap.

From the northern corner of the summit plateau Cofa Pike, your next objective, rises almost immediately below. Steep grass and scree lead down to it and in winter conditions care should be taken here. The further you trend to the left the easier the angle. The summit ridge of Cofa Pike gives an airy but easy scramble. From the saddle below and beyond this peak, Deepdale Hause, there is a fine view across Sleet Cove of Hutaple Crag. The discovery by Alf Gregory, the Everest climber, of the potential of this massive broken crag, shortly after the Second World War, opened up the rock-climbing possibilities of the eastern fells and began a wave of exploration.

A grassy ridge leads up to the rock-pimpled summit dome of St. Sunday Crag. You are now faced with two choices of descent. Either, head easterly along a well-defined ridge to the pointed summit of Gavel Pike. Beyond this follow a path twisting down the fell's eastern ridge to reach the footbridge over the Coldcove Gill near the entrance to Deepdale. Or, return down to Deepdale Hause and drop leftwards, down steep grass and scree, into the rugged environs of Sleet Cove, and leftwards again down into Deepdale. To return down the lush turf of Deepdale, with the serrated skyline of Fairfield imposed upon the evening sky behind, is a delight. Eventually a narrow high-walled lane leads onto the A592. Turn right and follow the grass verge to where a rocky step thrusts into the road. Cross this by a stile and follow a path through the wood, above and parallel to the road, back to the car park.

Walk 6   9 miles

Walna Scar, White Maiden and Caw

Coniston Old Man is one of the most well-trodden of Lakeland fells, and its neighbours Swirl How, Wetherlam and Dow Crag scarcely less so. The walk described below explores a less crowded corner of the Coniston group and its humbler, but nonetheless interesting, tops.

Parking: Park at the north end of Torver village at the foot of the lane leading up to Walna Scar, near the bridge over the Torver Beck. (GR 285945). A lay-by north of the bridge offers more space.

CLIMB up the lane following finger-posts inscribed 'Walna Scar'. Eventually the tarmac ends and the track becomes rougher and steeper. After passing through a gate near a ruined barn the angle eases and soon the path begins to descend. A fine view of Dow Crag and Coniston Old Man now opens up ahead. Soon a sign on a wall on your left points you to the right of Tranearth Cottage, a climbing hut, and towards the massive spoil heaps of Banishead Quarry. Below the spoil heaps pass through a gate, turn immediately right through a narrow passage, cross the bridge over the beck and follow the path through the spoil heaps to swing to the right of a huge man-made hole with a beck spilling over its far corner. Beyond the quarry climb steeply up alongside Torver Beck to reach the Walna Scar track near a bridge.

These moors below Walna Scar, sweeping down to Torver, reek with history and mystery. There are ancient cairns and enclosures and stories of 'giants' graves'. In a small stone circle just below the Walna Scar track Collingwood unearthed Bronze Age cremation urns containing the remains of a child aged 2 to 3 years. Years ago the photograph of a UFO, taken on these moors by a Coniston doctor's son, was splashed across the front pages of a national daily.

Cross the bridge and follow the Walna Scar track, with the towering fissured face of Dow Crag to your right. Quarried stone, iron-ore, wool-clips, salt, illicit whisky, fancy goods, all have been packed across this ancient mountain highway.

On the grassy saddle of Walna Scar ignore the cairned and worn path climbing right, up to Brown Pike, and climb left to the crest of a broad grassy ridge. Ahead of you the ridge splits into the summits of White Maiden and White Pike, with the prominent peak of Caw beyond them. Easy walking, with fine views on either hand, leads to the White Maiden cairn. Now follow a wall into a dip below White

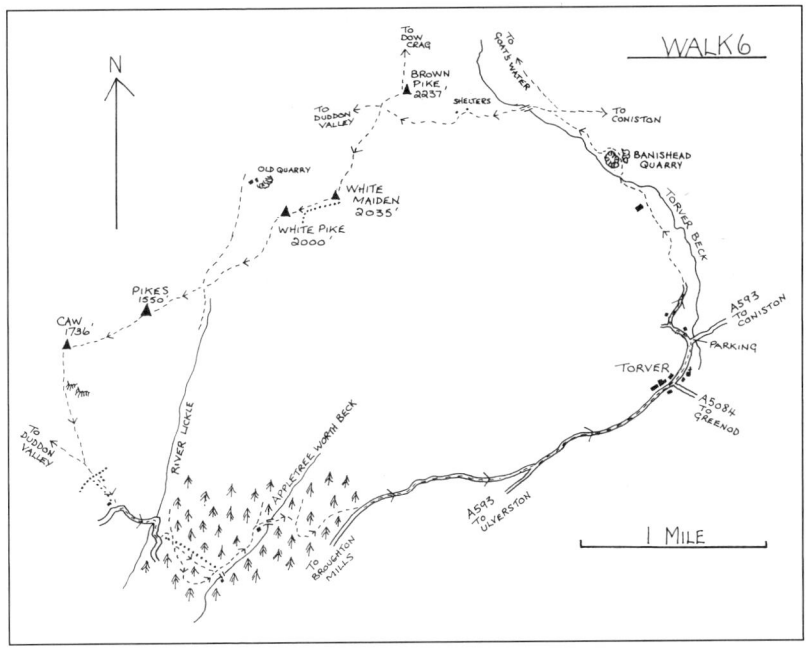

Pike before climbing up to capture this summit. South-westerly now rises the distinctive profile of Caw crowned by a prominent cairn and the nearer, but equally shapely, Pikes.

Now head south-westerly, down a surprisingly craggy fellside, into the wide saddle below Pikes. Climb Pikes by just picking a line and storming its steep, craggy flanks until you emerge on the narrow top. Looking back White Pike displays a rugged profile. Beyond rises Brown Pike, and its slanting scar of path, with Dow Crag to its left and Coniston Old Man rising between and beyond them. Left of Dow Crag are Swirl How and Great Carrs, and leftwards further the dome of Grey Friar. The great mass of the Scafells, and their mighty acolytes, lie beyond. Across Dunnerdale rises Harter Fell, with Devoke Water to its left.

Head south-westerly, down and up, to the trig-point on Caw. Beyond lie the gleaming waters of the Duddon estuary guarded by brawny Black Combe. Now descend into the valley beyond, picking a southerly way through broken crags. As you descend look for a wall to your left running across the valley, with a walled lane leading from it. Head for this lane and follow it down to a gate leading onto a tarmac road. Follow the road down, over a bridge, and up again into woodland. Leave it through a gate on your left marked 'Forestry Association' to join a forest road. Turn right along this rough road which shortly passes between an old wall. Some fifty yards beyond this wall a path leads into the trees on your left. It is indistinct and often blocked by fallen trees but if you keep the wall to your left you will eventually emerge onto a forest road above a ruined building and a footbridge over a beck. Your original forest road reaches the same point by a longer, circuitous curve.

Now turn left up the forest road until, beyond a turn left around a rocky corner, a path will be spotted heading down into the trees on your right. Follow this past buildings, across a concrete bridge over a beck and up to join a further forest road. Turn right here. Ignore any misgivings as it continues to swing right for eventually it veers left again and leads you out of the trees and onto a tarmac road. Turn left along this road which gives you fine views of the fells you have climbed. Look back to see Caw rising dramatically over the trees. A mile and a half of road walking brings you back to Torver.

Walk 7 **5 miles**

Coniston Old Man and Dow Crag via Raven Tor

This is a fine walk which reaches the summit of one of Lakeland's most well-trodden fells but by an interesting and apparently unfrequented ridge. It also crosses the summit of one of Lakeland's major climbing crags, giving the walker a bird's-eye view of climbers in action. Unfortunately the early part of the walk passes through the unsightly debris of industry, both ancient and modern. For those interested, however, this illustrates an important chapter in the history of Lakeland and one cannot help but have admiration for man's skill, courage and ingenuity in wresting riches from the obdurate rock.

Parking: In Coniston village car park or at the top of the lane running up from the Black Bull Hotel, just below the 'private road' signs. (GR 304975 or 301979).

WALK up this lane and the rough track beyond which eventually levels out into the Copper Mines Valley, passing above some fine cascades in Church Beck. At the entrance to the valley there is a bridge over the beck and a signpost indicating Coniston Old Man lies that way. Ignore this and continue straight ahead. The flat valley, its green flanks scarred and hacked and its floor piled with spoil heaps and ruined workings, is a desolate place. Only the brightly painted old miners' dwellings on the fellside, holiday cottages now, and the white walls of the youth hostel and the climbing hut ahead, enliven the scene. The bulk of the industrial scars and debris date from the decade 1854–1864, the period of peak production when around six hundred men and boys were employed here. We can, however, lift our eyes to a superb skyline — the Old Man, bearing man's cruel scars with dignity, Brim Fell, Swirl How and rugged Wetherlam.

Continue with the rough track past the youth hostel and the higher and partially buried modern pumping station. Then leave it and bear left to a footbridge spanning Levers Water Beck below a series of fine waterfalls. Cross the bridge and climb the path slanting across the spoil heaps spilling out of the grim dark portal of Simon's Nick. This path ends on the crest of the Levers Water dam. The scars of industry are left behind now and the eyes are soothed by graceful mountain shapes and the ears by the soft lap of water against stone. The dam is a well consructed piece of work, its flat grassy top making an ideal picnic and sunbathing spot and the boulders of its facing forming useful diving platforms.

The steep rocky spur of Raven Tor, thrusting out from the main Old Man–Swirl How ridge, towers above the south-western end of the dam. To reach it follow the crest of the ridge behind the dam to arrive at a grassy saddle below Raven Tor. From this ridge there is a fine view of yacht-speckled Coniston Water and the wooded hills of Furness rolling away towards the distant blue line of the Pennines and Ingleborough's pronounced hump. To the right of this ridge is the fenced-off chasm of Simon's Nick, reputedly a thousand feet deep. Simon was said to be in league with fairies who, in return for his trust, revealed to him hidden reefs of copper. When he betrayed their trust they caused him to be buried in his horrendous hole. There are other less awfully impressive but equally lethal shafts in the vicinity — so be wary of them. From the saddle below Raven Tor a path drops leftwards into Boulder Valley. You will probably be able to pick out the Pudding Stone below, the mighty monarch of the monoliths scattered about this rocky hollow.

From the saddle, climb up steep grass to reach the foot of the rocks of Raven Tor. Your choice of route is now wide open; pick your own line through the broken rocks above. The further left you go the steeper the ground, the further right the more amenable. All

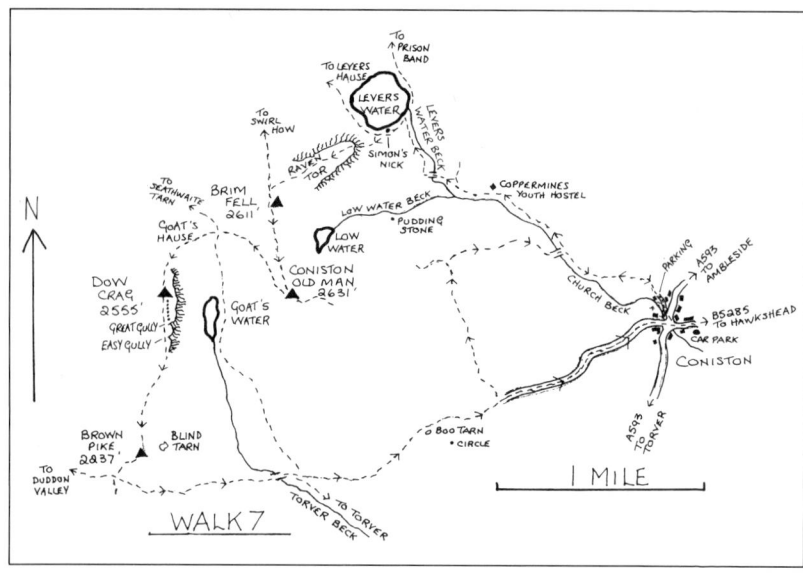

ways end on the broad grassy crest of the spur which undulates upwards to a junction with the main ridge just below and to the right of the summit cairn of Brim Fell. It is now an easy walk southwards, along a broad grassy ridge, to capture the summit of Coniston Old Man. As you go the strangely-blue depths of Low Water (something to with the quarrying?) lie below, to your left, whilst over the right-hand crest the spiky summit of Dow Crag slowly thrusts into view. A dip in your ridge reveals Dow Crag with the blue dot of the Mountain Rescue Box at its foot giving some idea of scale.

From the Old Man's cairn retrace your steps a short way to where a narrower path breaks leftwards, north-westerly. This slants across steepening grassy slopes, above the gloomy waters of Goats Water, and down to the broad grassy saddle of Goats Hause. Escape can be made here, if desired, by turning down to Goats Water and on to the Walna Scar track. To continue, climb up the rocky path, swinging leftwards, to reach the rocky tor whose highest rock is the summit of Dow Crag. Continue along the ridge, alongside an old wall at first, to where a great wedge is bitten out of it. This is the head of Great Gully and a circumspect peek over gives some idea of the height and steepness of the crag. A little further down the ridge, from the rim of Easy Gully, a safer aerial view may be had of climbers in action on climbs on the crag's 'A' and 'B' buttresses. Beyond Easy Gully the crag tails off and the slope below, though steep, is mainly grass and scree. Below now nestles Blind Tarn, so christened because it has no exit stream, the fourth lovely mountain tarn to be passed on this walk.

The ridge makes a final climb to cross the summit of Brown Pike before dropping down to Walna Scar Pass. Turn left here. Where this worn and ancient mountain highway crosses the bridge over the Torver Beck look left for an impressive view of Dow Crag at its baroque and darkly-cleft best. Just over half a mile further on the track passes to the left of a small, and often dry, tarn — Boo Tarn.

Upon reaching the gate where the tarmac road begins, and depending upon where you have parked your car, either follow the road down to Coniston or turn left and follow the rough quarry road to the first steep left-hand bend where a path veers right and down into the Copper Mines Valley.

Walk 8   **8 miles**

A Little Langdale Horseshoe

This horseshoe is inferior to its Great Langdale counterpart (Walk 18) only in that it requires less commitment and energy to complete it, being neither as long, as high, or its terrain as abrasive. Its peaks, however, are shapely, less crowded, and the views from them equally widespread and delightful. It is the varied and visible reminders, from huge man-made caverns, old mine workings and wrecked warplanes, of mankind's impact upon the fells that makes this walk particularly unique.

Parking: Take the minor road branching west off the Skelwith Bridge–Coniston road, the A593, about a third of a mile north of its highest point, at GR 329023. Branch right at the first, and immediate, fork and follow this for just over a mile to reach a footbridge and ford over the River Brathay. Park hereabouts. This footbridge can be reached from Little Langdale village by a narrow lane signposted 'Tilberthwaite Ghyll'. After one traumatic crossing I don't recommend attempting the ford — not in a Mini anyway!

FOLLOW the path past the bridge and alongside the river. After passing through a gate, slate spoil heaps will be seen to your left, and shortly afterwards a gate leading up into them. Go through this gate and climb up to the second terrace and a hut with a National Trust emblem on its door. Behind the hut is a rocky fissure crowned by a slate arch. Pass under the arch and follow the fissure (do not be deterred by the low wet tunnel seen ahead), until a hidden opening on the left leads to a dramatic view into a huge man-made cavern supported by a thick leaning pillar. **(Since writing this account I have visited this spot to find there's been a rock-fall into the fissure which has to be climbed over in order to view the cavern. The cavern is magnificent but obviously there is possible danger from falling rock).**

Return down to the original path and continue. After passing Low Hall Garth Farm and a climbing hut it narrows into a walled lane below slate spoil heaps, ending at a gate. Three hundred yards or so beyond the gate the path forks. Follow the left-hand path which heads towards the old mine workings guarding the entrance to Greenburn seen about a mile ahead. Away to your right the Langdale Pikes display themselves to rugged effect. The Greenburn mine workings are extensive, with one grim, body-wide and poorly fenced shaft which is in my reference files for the day I write my Lakeland who-dunnit. Beyond them, Greenburn Tarn, dammed to provide power, is a pleasant bathing and picnic site. Above the workings, on the slopes of Wetherlam, a path can be picked out zig-zagging up towards some obvious spoil heaps. This is another old 'sledgate' (see Walk 4); it will be your eventual line of descent.

Now cross the Greenburn Beck and climb up the far slope to reach the crest of Rough Crags. Looking back across Greenburn the 'sledgate' is a clearly visible scar on the flank of Wetherlam. Turn left now and plod up the amiably unrelenting ridge of Wet Side Edge. Below, to your right, the shining, multi-coloured beetles crawl up Wrynose Pass, put into their rightful place in the scheme of things by the splendour of the rugged fells rising above and beyond them. Where Wet Side Edge begins to climb steeply southwards towards the rocky summit of Great Carrs a path branches off south-westerly towards Grey Friar, an isolated and relatively unfrequented fell overlooking the Duddon valley. Peak-baggers please note that this may be added to the round with only a modicum of excess energy expenditure. South-westerly from the Great Carrs cairn, beyond Grey Friar, shapely Harter Fell overlooks the ubiquitous glinting beetles now toiling over Hardknott Pass.

Swirl How is easily reached by following the fell rim in a dipping and rising curve south then east. When just beyond the summit of Great Carrs look to your right for the wreckage of a Halifax bomber, marked in recent years by a wooden cross, which crashed here during the war, all the crew perishing. To your left an engine

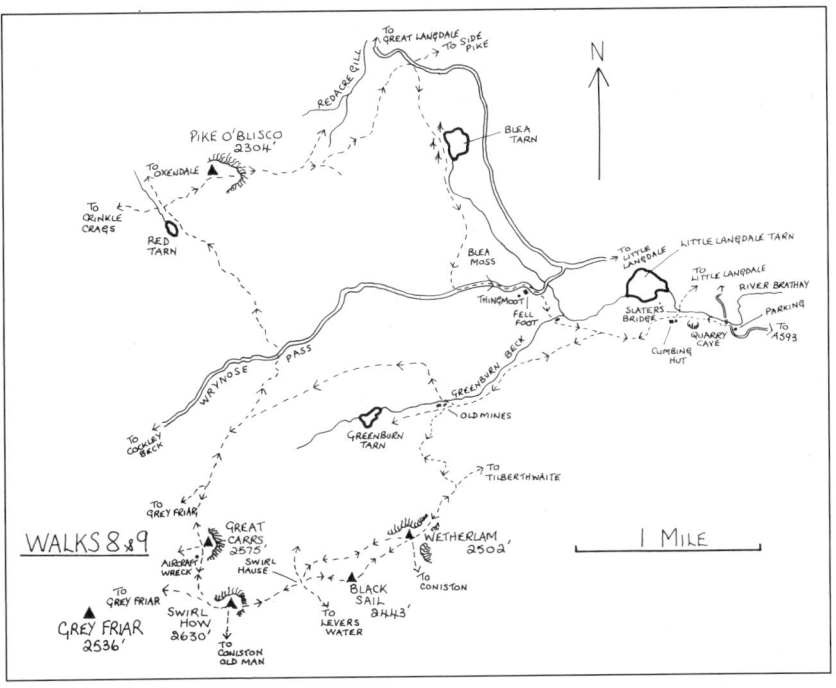

may be spotted spilled on the scree below. From the airily perched Swirl How cairn head easterly, bending north-easterly, down a fine rocky ridge, curiously named Prison Band, to the narrow, cairned, saddle of Swirl Hause. Levers Water and Coniston Water display themselves well from here. From Swirl Hause a good path climbs onto the northern rim of the Wetherlam massif and follows it around, easterly, to Wetherlam summit. Peak baggers beware that this path avoids the subsidiary summit of Black Sail.

Descend from Wetherlam by the north-east ridge, Wetherlam Edge. The upper section of this ridge is steep and rocky — care should be taken in bad conditions. Where the ridge eases off the path passes to the left of a pronounced rocky hump. Look left here, or in the dip beyond, for cairns which lead down to a spoil heap below an old tunnel and the beginning of the 'sledgate'. Return down this to the old Greenburn Mine buildings. Given the right sort of weather a fine finish to the day would be to cross the stone stile below Low Hall Garth Farm and go for a dip in one of the pools above or below the delightful, time-polished span of Slaters Bridge.

Walk 9

11 or 12 miles

Another Little Langdale Horseshoe

The Little Langdale Horseshoe described in the previous walk is really a Greenburn rather than a Little Langdale round. The walk described below seeks to correct this by adding length and interest to the quarry-cave, old mines, crashed warplanes, shapely peaks and delectable tarns already described.

Parking: As for Walk 8.

FOLLOW the directions given in Walk 8 as far as '. . . a path can be picked out zig-zagging up towards some obvious spoil heaps. This is another old 'sledgate'.' Now climb the 'sledgate'. It ends near a tunnel entrance but cairns continue upwards to bring you onto the crest of Wetherlam Edge near a pronounced and rounded outcrop of rock. A pleasant scramble follows to capture the summit of Wetherlam. Now the way lies south-of-west, edging around the north-western rim of the fell, to reach the narrow saddle of Swirl Hause. It adds variety, however, to keep above this path and bag the relatively unfrequented summit of Black Sails before descending to Swirl Hause. From here the eye leapfrogs down the aqueous splendours of Levers Water and Coniston Water.

A rocky ridge, curiously named Prison Band, which gives some pleasant scrambling if taken direct, leads up to the Swirl How cairn, perched dramatically on the tip of its northern prow. For Great Carrs, your next objective, simply follow the rim of the fell down and around, west then north. From the dip between the peaks, in my experience one of the windiest spots in Lakeland, look down onto the scree below to spot an engine of a wartime Halifax bomber which crashed just below and to the south-west of Great Carrs summit. All the crew perished in the impact which flung both engines over the crest and down into Greenburn. Just before reaching the summit look to your left for more wreckage, and in recent years a wooden cross, marking the site of the crash. From Great Carrs top the enthusiast may make a relatively easy diversion south-westerly to bag the isolated summit of Grey Friar. For details of the view from Great Carrs refer to Walk 8.

Leave Great Carrs, descending northwards and then veering north-easterly onto Wet Side Edge, curving back around Greenburn. Some three-quarters of a mile on a cairn marks a path fork. Turn left here and drop down steepening grass to reach the crest of Wrynose Pass. Now cross the road and take the path heading up into the gap between Cold Pike and Pike o'Blisco. This path climbs up to and passes the austere waters of Red Tarn.

Once on the saddle you are presented with the view featured on the front cover of *Fellwalking with Wainwright* — the craggy ramparts of the Crinkles echelon away towards rock-armoured Bowfell. Turn right here and climb the path heading up and into the rocky trench dividing Pike o'Blisco's two summits. Scramble left to the slabby highest point. The view ranges from shapely Skiddaw in the far north to lowly Black Combe in the south-west, beyond the gap of Hardknott Pass. Across the depths of Oxendale and Mickleden the rugged breast of Pike o'Stickle is slashed by the pale scar of Stone Axe Gully. To descend, bear left, eastwards, out of the rocky trench taking either of two paths. Both have awkward 'scrambly bits' through the belts of rock guarding the summit. They merge on the easier ground beyond and bring you to the head of Redacre Gill, the usual line of ascent or descent. Bear right here and follow a fainter path, away from the gill. When this forks keep to the left. This tenuous path twists around and down the ridge forming the eastern wall of Redacre Gill to meet the road linking Great and Little Langdale, via Blea Tarn, at its highest point.

Do not cross the road but turn right, over a stile, and head down towards Blea Tarn. Pass the tarn through a splendid tunnel of rhododendron bushes. At the end of this tunnel the path forks, your way lying ahead over a stile. (If, however, you feel like a dip or simply a look at the oft-photographed and painted view of the Langdale Pikes rising above Blea Tarn diverge left across the footbridge). Beyond the stile the path stays close to the beck, which plunges into a rocky ravine, before veering away to the right, around the edges of Blea Moss, to reach the Wrynose Pass road. Turn down this to eventually pass in front of Fell Foot Farm. The grassy mound rising behind the farm is reputedly a 'thing-moot', a kind of meeting place of the local parliament and a relic of the invasion of Lakeland by Norsemen in the tenth-century. Soon there is a packhorse bridge over the beck to your right. Cross this, go through the gate, and follow the path beyond to a further gate and bridge near a fine example of an old Lakeland farmhouse. Continue, to a junction with your outward route.

Variation: Another finish to this walk, and probably the completion of a true Little Langdale Horseshoe, would be to cross the Blea Tarn road at its highest point and continue over Side Pike and Lingmoor before descending to the valley and your car. I plan to try that one soon.

Walk 10 6 miles

Harter Fell, Mediobogdum and Dunnerdale

Harter Fell is an elegantly sculpted and isolated fell that is more of a mountain than others half its height again. Hardknott Castle (Mediobogdum) adds a flavour of history and romance to the walk, whilst Dunnerdale is as lovely, and only half as crowded, as any other Lakeland valley.

Parking: In the Dunnerdale Forest car park and picnic site a few hundred yards north of where Birks Bridge spans a foaming Duddon. (GR 235995).

CROSS the Duddon by the less elegant bridge near the car park. Follow a forest road, passing through a gate and gradually climbing leftwards. Where this road emerges from the trees a track branches left down to buildings. Continue with the forest road towards a gap in an old wall. Before reaching the gap bear right up a path climbing the bank near a red-ringed guide-post. Follow it through a gateway, into a boggy dip, and up into a gap between the trees. When the trees close in ahead look for a cairn in the trees on your left marking a parallel path. The way bears upward to the left now, either in the bouldery bed of an incipient beck or in the trees to its left. Both merge in a more open area to the left of a small crag. A little higher the path goes to the left of another crag and emerges onto the open fellside.

A prominent rock pinnacle, Maiden Castle on the large OS map, crowns the skyline ahead and the path crosses a stile over a fence to the right of it. Now the angle eases but the path becomes fainter if anything. It has a tendency to bear to the left of most of the rocky outcrops approached before eventually bearing right up to the summit. It doesn't really matter if you lose the path for this is an isolated peak and as long as you keep heading upwards you are bound to reach the top. Scramblers will find their fun keeping to the rock that thrusts generously through the grassy pelt of this fell and will be delighted with its delectable top. This is a great block of Borrowdale Volcanic, towering to the east of the faint-hearted trig point and making Harter Fell one of the rare Lakeland tops that can only be bagged by use of the hands as well as the feet.

The highlights of the view from Harter Fell are, for me, both to the north. Immediately below Mediobogdum straddles its spur, commanding Eskdale. Spread below you is the archetypal plan of

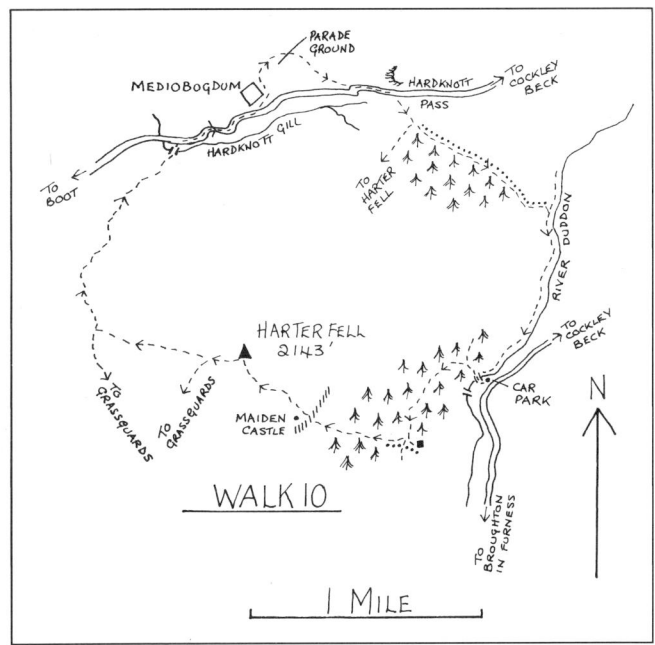

the Roman fort that remained unchanged for centuries and was planted on conquered soil from Persia to Perthshire. Now raise your eyes from a crumbling symbol of man's ever-violent history to the timeless magnificence of England's highest and wildest hills.

Now follow a path down a grassy groove to the left of the trig point. This north-of-westerly path is well worn, being the most popular way up and down the fell, albeit the most boring. Ignore a cairned diversion left shortly below the top. Continue down slanting rightwards, with Eskdale spreading away below, to reach a gate signposted 'Bridlepath/Hardknott'. Beyond this the path is wide and obviously built up and it leads easily down to the foot of Hardknott Pass. Skirting Harter Fell, linking Eskdale to Dunnerdale, it was once part of the network of roads that shuttled goods, animals and people across mountain Lakeland. Ahead, Bowfell, the quintessential mountain shape, towers elegantly above Upper Eskdale. A Lakeland Weisshorn.

Walk up Hardknott's corkscrewing grass verges to explore Mediobogdum. Although the actual ruins are not particularly impressive it must be one of the most dramatically situated military strongholds in the world. Surely the most hard-bitten legionary, or auxiliary, must have been impressed by the view from the ramparts as the seasons draped it in their coat of many colours. A levellish area above the fort is thought to have been the parade ground. Constantine the Great was the most famous of the several soldiers the legions of Britain raised to the purple in the chaotic centuries of the Late Empire. Perhaps one or more of these men served a tour of duty in this mountain stronghold, his words of command echoing back from the timeless crags above.

Follow the line of the old road curving under the crags of Border End to meet the tarmac road higher up. Climb this to a point just past the steep buttress of Raven Crag and beyond a culvert. Here a path branches off to the right. Follow it over a rise and through a gap in a wall before veering right, through a gap in another wall, to reach the corner of a plantation. Go down a soggy path between a wall and the trees. When the trees turn away continue down between the wall and a fence to the bank of the Duddon. Turn right and follow the river bank to reach the bridge back to the car park.

Walk 11   10 miles

The Scafells via the Great Moss

This is 'a walk on the wild side' of the Scafells, a connoisseur's way of reaching England's summit. Given the choice I prefer the 'shore' of the Great Moss to that of any of Lakeland's glamorous 'meres' or 'waters'. Here, under the loom of the Scafells and encircled by the rugged skyline of Esk Pike, Bowfell and Crinkle Crags, the heart beat of mountain Lakeland is almost palpable.

Parking: In the lay-by at the foot of Hardknott Pass, on the Eskdale side. (GR 214012).

WALK up the road until the wall on your left turns away. Now follow this wall to a stile in a wall corner. Beyond, follow the obvious path through gates and over stiles for about a mile to reach the bank of the Esk. Brotherikeld, the farm below the start of this section, was a flourishing sheep farm in the thirteenth century when the Cistercians held it.

Follow the river, passing one of Lakeland's finest bathing pools, to reach the sheep fold and packhorse bridge below the Throstle Garth waterfalls. This bridge, unlike many Lakeland 'packhorse bridges', is unadorned with the walls that would in reality have made it impossible for pack-train traffic. It has rightly been described as 'a timeless piece of vernacular architecture'. How many loaded pony trains, licit or illicit, must have crossed it, and how varied their loads! The lichened boulders of the nearby sheepfold must have been scoured by the sheep of centuries. The thirteenth century Lord of Millom saw Upper Eskdale as a hunting preserve. Knights and their ladies may have paused from the chase to refresh themselves by this junction of cascading water.

Cross the bridge and continue up the right bank of the Esk, which now carves a deep gorge below you. Ahead, England's stony roof at last begins to make its presence felt. First Ill Crag, interestingly double-topped with dome and cone, then the Pike itself, Mickledore, the shadowy bulges of the East Buttress, Scafell summit with the Cam Spout Buttress a downward curve of scree terrace and rock band, and the final gully-seamed spur of Slight Side, all march into view as height is gained.

The Esk eventually climbs up from the froth and foam of its rocky lair to burble amiably alongside you, twisting sharply left then right, to emerge onto the Great Moss.

The silver thread of Cam Spout waterfall, ahead and to your left, is now your target. The slabs to its right give some easy pleasant scrambling before the angle eases. The path climbs up the left-hand side of the combe ahead towards the obvious saddle of Mickledore. A few hundred feet below Mickledore and just below the bulging rocks of Scafell's East Buttress an obvious wide bouldery gully leads up to your left. Scramble up this and just beyond its crest reach the incipient waters of Foxes Tarn. Climb steeply rightwards up loose scree to reach the summit ridge of Scafell. A turn left down onto a grassy saddle followed by a short climb beyond brings the summit cairn. The view is extensive, and in particularly clear conditions it has been claimed that not only Scottish hills but those of Ireland and Wales can be seen. Indeed, there is a legend in climbing circles that Craig yr Ysfa, a Welsh crag, was discovered with the aid of a telescope by a climber on Scafell top.

If you have a steady head and fancy something sterner, continue past the bouldery gully up to a point just below Mickledore. Here a large flake of rock at the foot of the crags on your left hides the narrow entrance to Broad Stand. Broad Stand is a serious scramble, formerly classified as a 'moderate' rock climb. The poet Coleridge is credited with the first descent, in 1802, and the epic left him with a severe case of 'shaky leg' and an eruption of 'heat bumps'. I've never managed it, up or down. Even when I was climbing regularly I never fancied it without a rope, and I've always been too

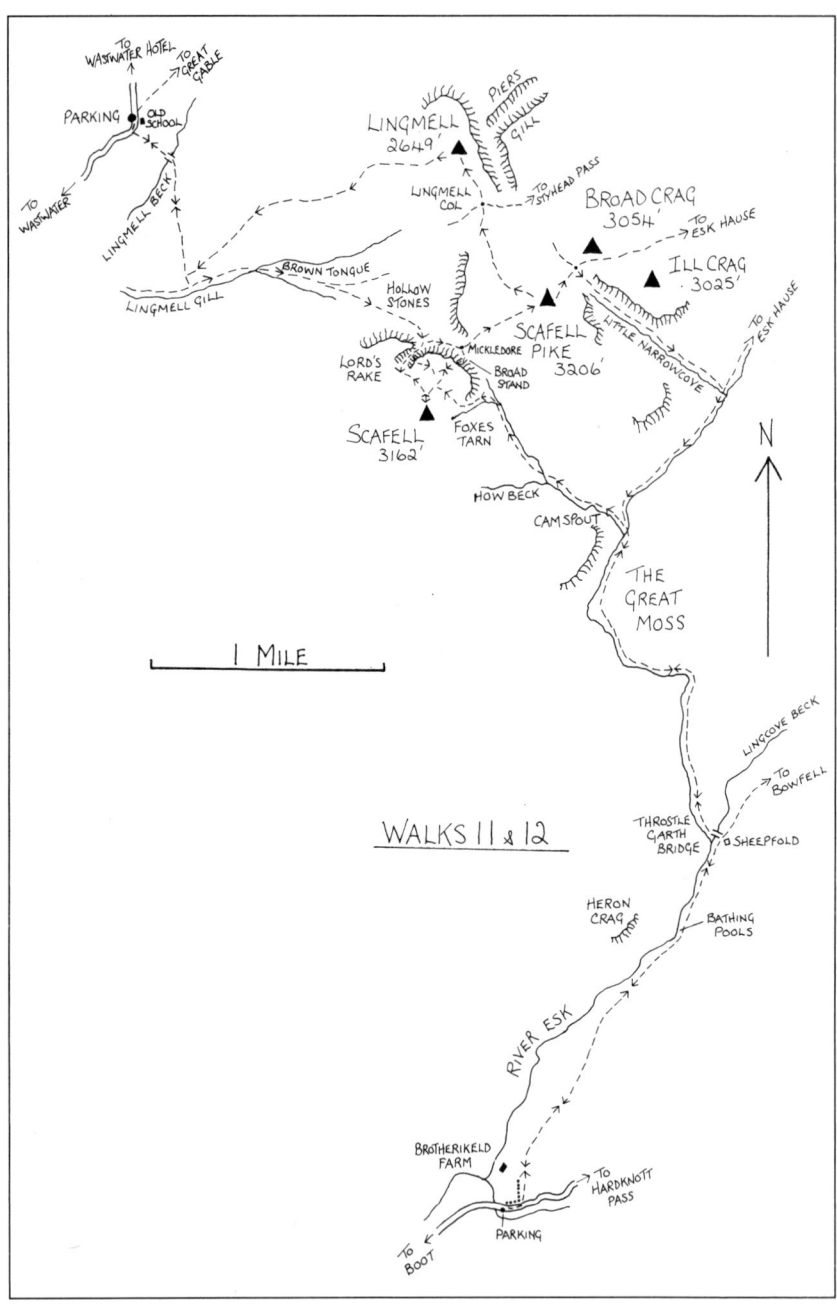

shamefaced to bring one for the attempt.

From Scafell, the most direct way to Scafell Pike is obviously by Broad Stand — enough said! Otherwise, from the grassy saddle bear left down a stony slope which drops away rightwards into Red Ghyll. Bear down a scree shoot into Red Ghyll which is defined on its left by an obvious slabby rock climb known as 'The Bannister'. The path climbs out of the ghyll to a narrow col, then dips again and up to a second narrow col at the crest of Lord's Rake. Slither down Lord's Rake with care. Its surface is deteriorating rapidly per every hundred pairs of boots that scrabble up or down it.

Carved in the rock at the foot of Lord's Rake is a cross marking the site where four climbers fell to their deaths in 1903. This was to be the worst climbing accident in Britain until five climbers were killed on Ben Nevis in 1954.

Turn right and follow the base of Scafell Crag up to reach the crest of Mickledore. The walker who has read something of the exploits of Lakeland's pioneer climbers will be able to pick out some of the physical features of the classic pioneering climbs on the gaunt rocks above. The Great Flake protrudes from the steep smooth walls of Central Buttress and was the key to unlocking 'CB', which reigned as the hardest climb in Britain for decades. Beyond 'CB' rears Botterill's Slab, probably the most pronounced feature on the face. It is like the pale edge of a giant book protruding from a vast library shelf. On the first ascent and at a moment he was having some difficulty, Botterill was asked by a lady and gentleman on the scree below 'if there was a way up there'. His difficulties increased as he attempted to fulfil the bounds of Edwardian propriety by raising his hat to the lady! His contemporary, the Lakeland climber and photographer George Abraham, suggested a strong gymnasium net should be permanently fixed below Botterill's Slab! From Mickledore, that 'hyphen' as Coleridge christened it, the way to Scafell Pike is obvious and dull work indeed after what has gone before.

From the man-trap boulders of England's summit, head northeasterly along the broad 'trod' leading eventually to Esk Hause. In the first deep dip, Broad Crag Col, turn right and descend into Little Narrowcove. This rocky gullet biting deep into the stony vitals of Scafell Pike is a delightful mountain sanctuary, with a score of superb lonely campsites guarded by towering pinnacles and crags. Little Narrowcove Beck joins the Esk near an old sheep fold. Turn right and follow the river, passing under the sheer walls of Esk Buttress, first climbed on in the 1920s, to join your outward route below Cam Spout.

Walk 12   **6 miles**

Scafell, Scafell Pike and Lingmell

This is a jewel of a mountain walk, packed with variety and interest in its few miles. In the course of it England's highest summit is climbed, although this is plain fare indeed after the 'hors d'oeuvres' of the magnificent rock scenery of Scafell. Mountaineering and even literary history play their part here too. On Scafell Crag some great feats of early British mountaineering were enacted. Herford, Botterill, Owen Glynne-Jones, are just a few of those who created legends. The poet Coleridge tentatively and bravely slithered down a first descent of Broad Stand in 1802, a remarkable tour-de-force considering the psychological attitudes of the times towards mountains. Scramble about these crags and, be they warmed by the sun or shredding the racing clouds on their topmost points, it is a dull mind that feels no stirring of the spirit.

Parking: In Wadale Head, on the green near the old schoolhouse. (GR 187086).

WALK back a little way along the road to a stile, on the left, signposted 'The Scafells'. Cross it and follow the path across the fields to a footbridge over Lingmell Beck. The path now slants right, passing through several stiles, climbing around a spur of Lingmell. A junction with the path coming up from Brackenclose and the campsite is made on the bank of the Lingmell Gill. The path now climbs alongside the gill, crossing it eventually where it splits at the foot of the steep grass ridge called Brown Tongue (GR 196075). The Tongue is climbed and beyond it the path forks. The left-hand fork is more worn and prominently cairned and leads to the Lingmell–Scafell Pike col and eventually the summit of the latter peak. Now head right, however, in the direction of the crags and cross a turfy section, passing a well-marked hollow filled with boulders on the left. The whole of this area is known as Hollow Stones. The approach to Scafell is slightly left up a green ridge on the right of a well-marked watercourse (often dried up in summer) to a large boulder at the top of Hollow Stones.

Now head towards the hollow between Scafell and Pikes Crags. Scafell Crag, on the right, looks more impressive with every upward step, and to the stranger it must seem impossible that there is a way for fell walkers through this barrier. Upon reaching the scree bear right up it to the base of the crags and the key to Fortress Scafell will be revealed — Lord's Rake, a steep scree gully slanting up through the crags. Scramble with care up the loose surface of the Rake, passing to the right of a shallow cave formed by a large wedged boulder. This is the entrance to Deep Ghyll. The crest of Lord's

Rake is a narrow rocky col. Just below this a path slants left, with a couple of airy steps, to debouch onto the scree funnel of upper Deep Ghyll. This path is known as the West Wall Traverse and provides a more direct route to the summit. From the head of Deep Ghyll a short walk to the south, across a grassy saddle, reaches the summit cairn.

To continue with Lord's Rake, beyond the col a short drop and rise leads to a similar mountain notch. Beyond this a longer descent and subsequent climb is made across Red Ghyll to emerge onto the stony western flank of the mountain. Turn left here and climb up to reach the summit ridge at a grassy saddle. Turn right to reach the cairn. (For the highlights of the view see Walk 11).

The most direct route to Scafell Pike from Scafell is by way of Broad Stand. For the reasons stated in Walk 11 I am in no position to recommend this route so must advise you to return to the foot of Lord's Rake by whichever route you came up. From there turn right and scramble along the base of Scafell Crag to reach the crest of Mickledore. (For descriptions of some of the physical features of Scafell Crag, and its history, see Walk 11). The last time we passed this way one of my friends stumbled across a lost £5 note, shivering without a survival wallet. My suggestion that all such waifs and strays should be placed in the care of the elder statesman of the party was received with abuse. From Mickledore the worn 'trod' up through the piled boulders crowning England's summit is dull work indeed after what has gone before.

Every time I revisit Scafell Pike's massive cairn I recall standing by it in the dawn of Coronation Day, June 1953. We had come up to celebrate the new reign by seeing the sunrise from England's summit. Instead we shivered in swirling mist and snow! There must have been other patriotic loonies about, however, for on the cairn two tiny Union Jacks, the kind children stick on sand castles on the beach, flapped bravely in the wind.

Now head generally north-west down to the grassy saddle below Lingmell, Lingmell Col. A short steep climb captures this relatively unfrequented peak and its graceful cairn. Lingmell is worth the extra effort for the spectacular view of Gable's hoary breast bloodied by deep furrows and criss-crossed by old scar tissue of paths. There are also airy glimpses down into Piers Ghyll and the ramshackle pinnacles overlooking it. Descend south-westerly down a grassy shoulder to join your outward route.

Walk 13　　　　　　　　　　　　　　　　　　　　　10 miles

The Mosedale Horseshoe

Fell walking seldom figures as a vehicle for drama, although real-life drama, exciting and tragic, frequently unfolds upon the crags and ridges of Lakeland. A few years ago a fine television play *The Mosedale Horseshoe*, written by Arthur Hopcraft, was produced by the BBC. Little was seen of the actual horseshoe, probably because of technical difficulties, and anyway the play was basically about human relationships, but if one had to choose a Lakeland walk that would be suitable for dramatic treatment this round of fine hills surrounding the bleak valley of Mosedale would take some beating.

Parking: The National Trust car park at the foot of Yewbarrow's south-west ridge. (GR 168068).

YEWBARROW actually turns its back on Mosedale, presenting its finest aspect towards Wastwater, but the horseshoe done properly should include it. Take the path up the ridge — a gruelling start! When a stile over the wall to your left is reached cross it and follow the path flanking along the fellside to where it forks. Take the right-hand path heading towards the steep buttresses of Dropping Crag. This path goes up a shaly gully to the right of the crag and emerges onto the ridge at the Great Door, an impressive rocky cleft in which the Scafells are dramatically framed. Steep climbing now leads onto the surprisingly broad and grassy summit ridge and the southern, and highest, cairn. Easy walking leads to the northern summit, but beyond this the character changes and some steep but easy scrambling has to be negotiated before the saddle of Dore Head is reached.

A stiff pull now reaches a big cairn crowning the southern shoulder of Wasdale Red Pike. This cairn is sometimes referred to as The Chair — for obvious reasons. The summit lies further on, marked by a small cairn perched on the lip of the precipitous flank overlooking Blackem Head. Keep to the crest here and not the path 'flunking' across the fell's western flank. This is what it's all about and you can't say you've done the Mosedale Horseshoe if you avoid all the graft. From the grassy saddle beyond, a faint path slants left down to Scoat Tarn and another, more obvious, path flanks, or 'flunks', right towards Wind Gap. Ignore this latter path and head directly up the fellside to reach the wall crowning the crest of Scoatfell. The tiny summit cairn is balanced on the top of the wall.

Climb over the wall and follow it leftwards to where a cairn stands

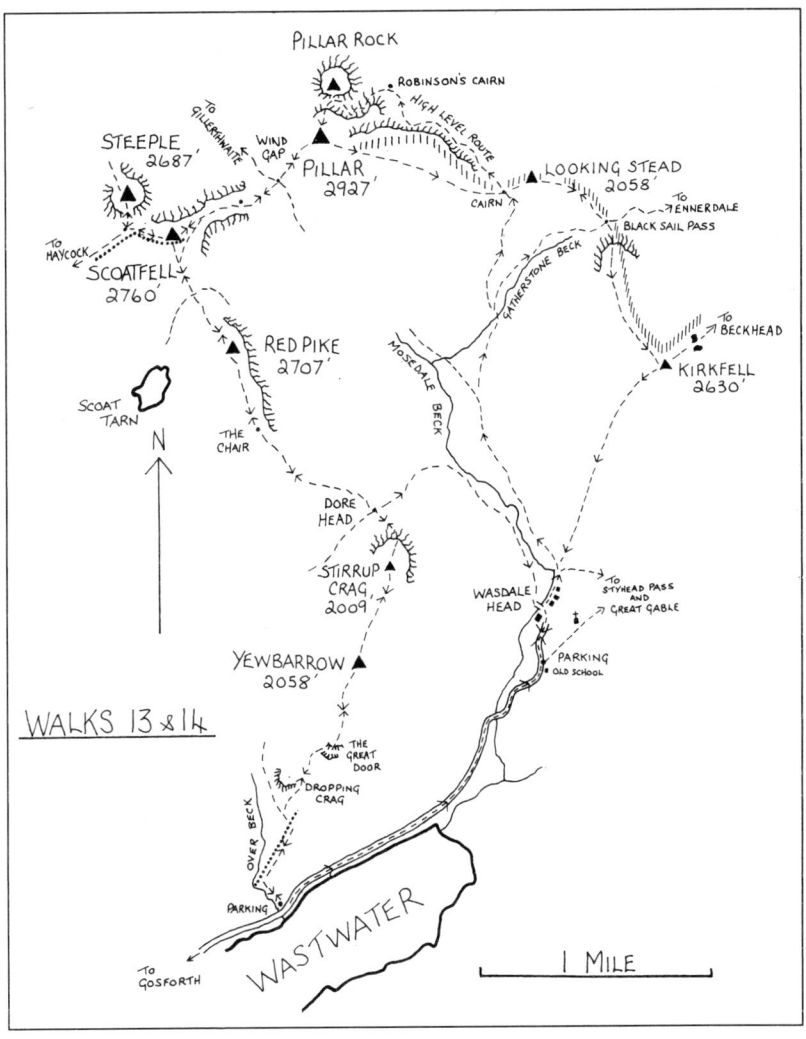

near it. Head north and down from this to capture the shapely outlying summit of Steeple. The vast gulfs of air filling rugged Mirklin and Mirk Coves on either hand of its narrow summit bear testimony to the aptness of its name. Return to Scoatfell summit.

Head north-easterly, following the wall at first. This soon ends and a bouldery descent leads onto a pleasant grassy ridge which ends with the bouldery summit and cairn of Black Crag. Beyond, a steep and stony descent leads to Wind Gap. By turning right here an escape can be made to Wasdale Head, if desired. To continue, a steep five hundred foot rocky scramble reaches the broad grassy summit of Pillar Mountain, the highest point of the horseshoe.

Descend the long easy south-east ridge to Black Sail Pass, bagging the outlying Looking Stead en route. From just beyond the trig-point, old fence posts take a circuitous but scenic line along the northern rim of the ridge with a more direct path lying slightly to the south. Black Sail Pass gives a further opportunity for escape should the weather deteriorate or enthusiasm wane.

To continue, the old fence posts lead in a steep but enjoyable scramble up the northern corner of Kirkfell. When the angle eases continue with the fence posts to reach the fell's western and highest summit. The view from Kirkfell is extensive in every direction save easterly, where Gable majestically fills the sky, a thrusting dome of naked rock and scree upon which the worn trods of men seem but the scrawls of a frail child.

Now head south-easterly to where a cairn marks the start of two thousand feet of steep knee-jellying grass. The good thing about this descent is that it finishes almost directly at the bar door of the Wastwater Hotel, where a refreshing pint will set you up for the march back up the road to your car.

Walk 14   **7 or 10 miles**

Pillar via the High Level Route

The High Level Route is the most interesting and exciting way for the fell walker to climb Pillar Mountain. Like walk-cum-scrambles of a similar nature on Gable and Bowfell, it was initially a climbers' path to the foot of their climbs which has become a popular fell walkers' way. To finish over Scoatfell, Red Pike and Yewbarrow gives a mountain day as good as anything Lakeland can offer.

Parking: As for Walk 12.

WALK up the lane to the Wastwater Hotel. Beyond and above the hotel, Pillar is a vast bulk blocking Mosedale. Go to the right of the hotel and turn right behind cottages to follow the right bank of the Mosedale Beck, passing a fine packhorse bridge. The path climbs up towards the foot of the grassy south-west ridge of Kirkfell, a grinding two thousand foot slog that must be one of the steepest climbs in Lakeland. Here the ways divide, a path bearing right to head towards Gavel Neese, the great prow of Gable and an equally intransigent climb.

Your route bears left, squeezed along with Mosedale Beck between Kirkfell and the craggy northern ramparts of Yewbarrow, which overlook the pale fans of the Dore Head screes. As you penetrate further into it the view opens up to your left as the valley thrusts an arm, Black Comb or Blackem Head, into the craggy guts of Wasdale Red Pike and Scoatfell. A path branches leftwards in this direction aiming for Wind Gap. Ignore this. Shortly afterwards your route begins to climb up the right bank of Gatherstone Beck, eventually crossing it and reaching the crest of a prominent spur, Gatherstone Head.

The cairn marking the start of the High Level Route stands on Pillar's south-east ridge and the path from Black Sail Pass, in a dip beyond the outlying summit of Looking Stead. To reach this cairn from Gatherstone Head you can either continue up to Black Sail Pass and subsequently the summit path, or take the shorter but steeper path that may be seen slanting across the fellside above and to your left.

The High Level Route debouches onto the fell's precipitous northern flank and traverses delightfully across the craggy slopes of Green and Hind coves to reach Robinson's Cairn. The original cairn, since unbelievably vandalised, was erected early in the century by members of the Fell and Rock Club as a memorial to J. W. Robinson of Lorton. Robinson played an important pioneering role in the early days of Lakeland climbing, especially on Pillar Rock, of which he was reputed to have made a hundred ascents. A photograph in a Fell and Rock Journal shows bowler-hatted and knickerbocker-breeched members and their floppy-hatted and voluminous-skirted ladies gathered near the inaugural cairn. There are one or two sections between Looking Stead and the cairn which must have given the ladies food for thought in their attire, and doubtless many a moustachioed stiff upper lip twitched and trembled at the flashing of a shapely ankle or two.

The first-time walker might look askance at the continuation of the High Level Route from the cairn — I did! A clear diagonal scrawl, the Shamrock Traverse, it looks as if the rocks above push it to the dizzy rim of the Shamrock. In fact there is little to worry about. It leads pleasantly, if airily, to the fellside behind Pillar Rock from where steep scree and grass lead to the summit of the mountain. Hard winter conditions, however, must make a different story of the High Level Route.

Viewed from Robinsons's Cairn, Pillar Rock gives an overriding sense of massive columnar strength. It can be clearly seen that the Rock has a lower and upper summit, or Low Man and High Man in climbers' parlance. The cleft to the left of High Man is known as the Jordan Gap and the rocky eminence on its farther side is Pisgah. The Rock appears to extend along the fellside towards the watcher near Robinson's Cairn. This nearer crag, however, is known as the Shamrock or Sham Rock, being separated from the Rock proper by a vertical cleft known as Walker's Gully. The unfortunate Walker was a seventeen-year old youth who on Good Friday, 1893, went to the aid of a party in difficulty near the Jordan Gap. He slipped on the snow, was unable to control his slide and pitched into the depths of the gully which as long as men climb will bear his name. The Rock was first climbed in 1826 by John Atkinson, a local man described as a 'cooper'.

To reach the start of the Shamrock Traverse follow the path to the left and over a low but noticeable rock barrier into the Great Doup, or Pillar Cove. Climb up this to where an obvious scree-shoot leads to the start of the Traverse.

England's highest mountain displays itself well from Pillar top. With Scafell in the vanguard, Broad Crag, Ill Crag, Bowfell and Great End march in sturdy file behind their monarch. All are challenged by the domed thrust of Gable, like some aggressive pretender to the throne.

Now head south-westerly down a steep and rocky ridge into the high saddle of Wind Gap and almost immediately up again in a steep bouldery climb to the cairn of Black Crag. A pleasant grassy ridge follows, dividing the isolated and craggy combs of Mirk Cove and Blackem Head, which culminates in a short bouldery scramble to the summit of Scoatfell. The small cairn is balanced on the wall that crowns this fell's broad summit. If you are feeling energetic continue along the wall to see a cairn close to it. Diverge north here to capture the shapely and airy summit of Steeple, and return.

From Scoatfell head south-westerly into the saddle below Red Pike. Continue over this fine fell, keeping to the summit ridge, which falls precipitously into Blackem Head, and not the path which flanks, or flunks, along its western slope. Dore Head is the saddle beyond Red Pike and a return to Wasdale Head can be made, if desired, by slithering left down the Dore Head screes. A more arduous but much more interesting finish is to continue with the scrambly up-and-over traverse of Yewbarrow. Although this entails an extra mile and a half of road walking at the end of the day the view of the Scafells framed in the walls of The Great Door, a rocky cleft below the southern summit, and the bird's-eye view of Wastwater make it worthwhile.

Walk 15 **9 miles**

Glaramara via the Cam Crag Ridge

The Cam Crag Ridge is a broad buttress of sun-catching pale rock, six hundred feet high, upon which 'scrambles' of varying degrees can be worked out. A delightful way to climb Glaramara. The logical start for the walk-cum-scramble is undoubtedly Stonethwaite in Borrowdale. This route is slightly shorter, less arduous, and has the added bonus of a dip in the superb natural swimming pool of Black Moss Pot at the end of the day, should the weather suggest it. We did it from Langdale, both to save driving and for something different, which made it harder for my middle-aged knees but easier on my passengers' nerves.

Parking: From time immemorial walkers and climbers have parked in the car park by the side of the Old Dungeon Ghyll Hotel, Great Langdale. Recently signs saying 'Parking for Bar Patrons Only' have been displayed. As most walkers invariably seek liquid refreshment after their endeavours I assume by this they are covered. (GR 286062).

GO behind the hotel, cross the stile and follow the stony track that eventually debouches onto the grassy flats of Mickleden. Above you the blunt prow of Gimmer Crag cleaves the Lakeland sky and conical, rock-girt Pike o' Stickle towers over the deep pallid furrow of Stone Axe Gully.

Beyond the footbridge at the end of Mickleden a slate marker near a sheepfold bears the legend '◀Esk Hause/Stake Pass▶'. Turn right and follow the steep path zig-zagging up the left bank of Stake Gill. Eventually the angle eases and the path crosses the beck to work around the right flank of a drumlin-dimpled hollow to reach the true crest of Stake Pass near a cairn. The major part of the walk can now be seen. The upper section of Cam Crag Ridge thrusts up a serrated skyline with the undulating Glaramara–Allen Crag ridge marching away to its left.

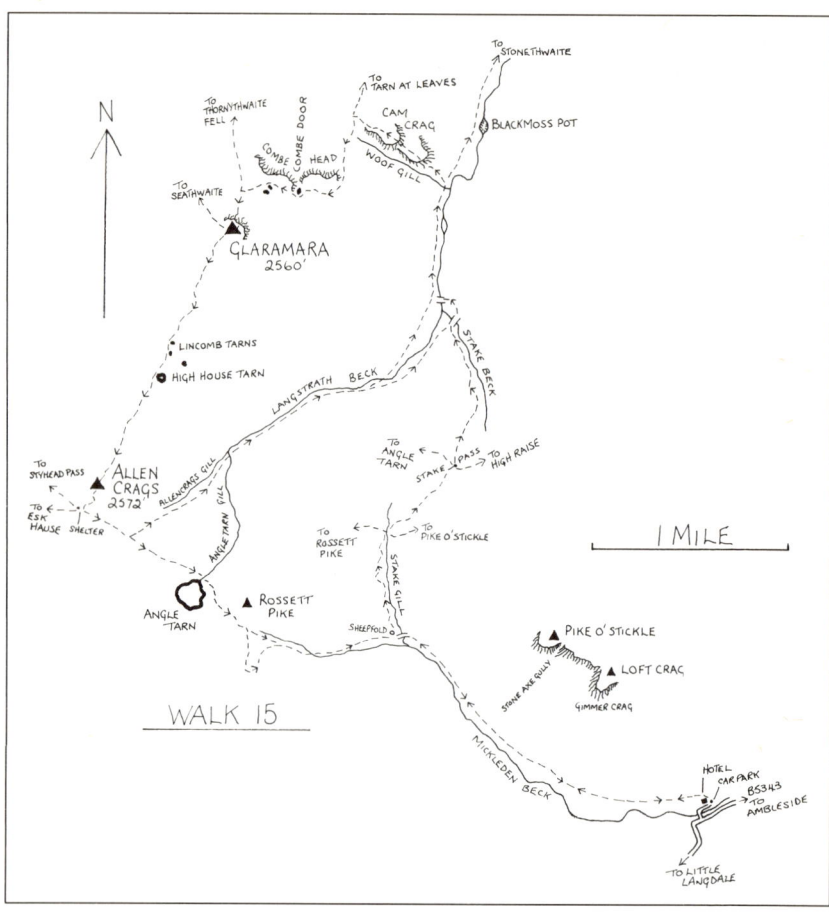

Follow the path down several easy-angled twists until a turn left brings a steepening of the ground and a splendid bird's-eye view of Langstrath. Cam Crag Ridge can now be seen in its entirety. Drop down grassy zig-zags alongside the rocky and splendidly cascaded Stake Beck and eventually cross it by a footbridge. Now angle towards another footbridge crossing the Langstrath Beck above a lovely bathing pool. The Langstrath Beck strings many fine pools along its meandering length but the one at Black Moss Pot, a quarter of a mile north of the foot of Cam Crag Ridge, must vie with the Throstle Garth pools to be crowned Lakeland's best. The Lakeland artist, W. Heaton-Cooper, has painted it, which must bestow the aesthetic accolade.

The southern flank of Cam Crag Ridge falls steeply into the ravine of Woof Beck. Walk down-valley and after crossing this beck head up steep brackeny slopes to the foot of the rocks. The first recorded ascent was by Bentley Beetham in 1943. Many climbers have found enduring fame in the annals of Lakeland climbing by discovering new climbs, some even new crags, but has anyone else ever discovered, practically single-handed, a whole new climbing ground? Beetham, a member of an early Everest expedition, did this with his 1953 edition of the Borrowdale climbing guide. The bulk of the climbs in its pages were solo first ascents due to a dearth of companions in a wartime Britain. Some of his creations were superb climbs, others bizarre, but always amusing and entertaining. The buttress is broad enough to offer a variety of lines of differing degrees of difficulty. Go as the fancy takes you.

The scrambling culminates in an undulating ridge, the last rocky pinnacle of which is a grand spot for a breather. Immediately beyond and below, the slabs of Raven Crag, another Beetham playground, curve impressively out of the depths of Combe Gill, whilst above and beyond Pillar and High Stile dominate. To your left the craggy ramparts of Combe Head hide Glaramara's summit.

The crest of Combe Head is reached by bearing left (south) along a broad humpy ridge, then climbing right (west) behind and above the crags and across the boggy, tarn-crowned notch of Comb Door. From Combe Head the rocky summit tor of Glaramara rears close. Head directly for it or continue west to meet the 'tourist' route from Borrowdale, via Thornthwaite Fell.

Superimposed on the rugged backcloth of Bowfell, Esk Pike, Ill Crag and Great End are Allen Crags. The mile and a half to this summit is a delightful, undulating high level walk around and over rocky tors and past a succession of superbly situated mountain tarns. From Allen Crags, Great End, cleaved by its trio of gullies, towers above Sprinkling Tarn. The Napes Ridges are starkly profiled on the steep sanguine breast of Gable, with plebian Kirkfell, and the Mosedale fells, beyond.

Now head easily down to the stone shelter below Esk Hause, the Picadilly Circus of Lakeland. Turn left here. Those heading for Langdale continue with the 'trod' down past Angle Tarn and onto the treadmill of Rossett Gill. Those Stonethwaite bound turn left in the first dip and follow a faint cairned path down the steep right bank of Allen Crags Gill into Upper Langstrath. Continue on to Stonethwaite, with perhaps a dip in the chilled, greeny, rock-girt depths of Black Moss Pot as a bonus en route.

Walk 16　　　　　　　　　　　　　　　　　　　　　8 miles

Ullscarf, Greenup Edge and High Raise

Rising almost slap bang in the centre of mountain Lakeland, Ullscarf and High Raise could both be loosely described as stowaway Pennine 'puddens'. It is highly unlikely that either would figure in most fellwalkers list of top twenty, or even fifty, favourite Lakeland fells. Nevertheless, there is much of interest in the views from their summits and the variety of terrain and scenery their sprawling flanks offer.

Parking: The National Trust car park just north of the bridge over Dob Gill on the western shore of Thirlmere. (GR 317139).

CROSS the stile at the rear of the car park and climb the path through the woods following the right bank of Dob Gill. When Harrop Tarn is reached leave this path and cross the stepping stones where Dob Gill issues from the tarn. Walk round the tarn until the first beck is met. Turn up this and follow it through the trees and out onto the open fell until Ullscarf Gill splashes down from your right to meet it. Now follow Ullscarf Gill.

There are no recognised paths on this flank of the fell. Generally the angle is easy, the ground boggy at times and in thick mist it could be a confusion of rocky tors, dead-end becks and glutinous sumps, but it has its own peculiar charm. You are unlikely to see a long crawling centipede of multi-coloured cagoules as yet another school party hits the fells, or find coke and beer cans or cigarette packets squashed under the boulders you sit on to have your sandwiches. You might, however, spot deer, or a fine fox lolloping over the bogs. Follow your own line south-westerly and eventually you will come out on Ullscarf's broad roof-tree somewhere near the cairn. A faint path following rusty relics of an old boundary fence will lead you to it.

Features of the view are a glimpse of the Solway beyond Bassenthwaite Lake, the stark profile of Honister Crag, Great End's trio of gullies, and a close and detailed view of the towering, gill slashed western flanks of Helvellyn. Follow the fence and path south, then south-westerly, in a gentle but somewhat moist descent to Greenup Edge.

This is an ancient Lakeland highway. Across it the Borrowdale monks sent to the mother-house, wool clips, dairy produce from

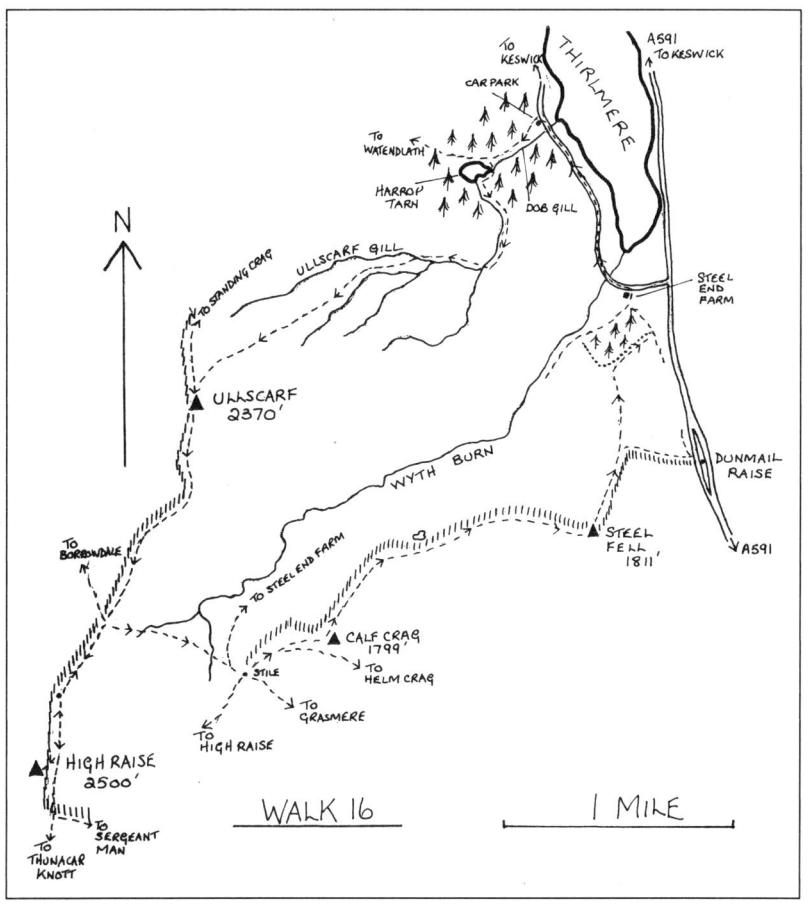

their 'vaccary' at Stonethwaite, salt from their Manesty spring, and iron from the bloomery on Smithymire Island at the confluence of Greenup Gill and Langstrath Beck.

Cross the path and bear up boggy slopes, still accompanied by fence remnants, to reach the rocks of Low White Stones. The angle eases and shortly more rocks are reached. Beyond these bear right, away from the fence, to reach the cairn and trig point of High Raise, sometimes called High White Stones.

Return to Greenup Edge. Turn right and follow the path down and across the back of the boggy hollow forming the head of Wythburn. Cross the headwater of the Wyth Burn and climb up to the grassy saddle, crowned by an isolated and rusting iron stile, that marks the head of Far Easedale.

Turn left here. Ignore the path curving away to the right, below the crest of the ridge and overlooking Far Easedale. Keep to the crest of the ridge, where occasional rusting fence posts mark the way, and follow it around, eastwards, to reach the summit of Calf Crag.

From here head north, at first, to follow a boggy ridge and fence posts curving easterly around the unfrequented valley of Greenburn, passing a sizeable unnamed tarn, to reach the summit of Steel Fell — worth the visit for the unique head-on view of Thirlmere.

Descend the fell's northern ridge to reach the corner of a plantation. Go down to the right, alongside the plantation, to reach the footpath from Dunmail Raise to Steel Fell Farm. Turn left towards the farm and road, then left again to finish.

Walk 17 **5 miles**

Harrison Stickle via Dungeon Ghyll

THE Langdale Pikes must be known to a high percentage of this country's population. People who have never set foot on a fellside must be familiar with the rugged skyline that has graced untold calendars, Christmas cards and book covers. They were the first mountains I ever climbed, some thirty years ago, and undoubtedly many walkers hold them in that same sentimental regard. The walk described below strikes a happy medium between the exposed scramble of Jakes Rake and the worn tourist 'trods'. It involves some mild scrambling but all real difficulties can be avoided. An entertaining route through imposing ravines and past fine waterfalls.

Parking: The free car park (sign) just beyond the entrance drive to the New Dungeon Ghyll Hotel. (GR 295065).

LEAVE the car park by stiles to join a well-worn path climbing leftwards from the New Dungeon Ghyll Hotel. Turn left to a kissing-gate. Beyond this turn right, passing a bench, to reach a second kissing-gate. Pass through this, cross the beck and take the well-worn path on its left bank. After a short climb a path will be seen slanting down to the right into the bed of the ghyll and the entrance of the rocky shaft containing Dungeon Ghyll Force. Stepping carefully and depending upon the amount of water coming down it is possible to enter the gloomy rift and peer up at the waterfall. Coleridge, himself an enthusiastic fell walker, is reputed to have modelled the 'deep romantic chasm' in his poem 'Kubla Khan' on Dungeon Ghyll Force. Arthur Dolphin, one of the great British rock climbers, celebrated this by naming one of his hard routes on Pavey Ark 'Alph', after the 'sacred river' featured in the poem.

Climb back out and continue with the original path until yet another path slants down into the bed of the ghyll, above the force. Go down this and now follow the beck, picking the easiest line, to where it turns right to a fine hidden waterfall. Scramble up the left bank of the fall to enter a splendid rocky gorge. Follow its fascinating twists and turns for about a mile, which entails some enjoyable scrambling from bank to bank, to reach the foot of a lovely high fall cascading into a rock basin. Circumvent this by scrambling to the left up a damp and crumbly gully.

Now follow the beck across easier ground. Loft Crag and Harrison Stickle now tower impressively ahead, with the craggy crest of Pavey Ark thrusting over the skyline to your right. Soon the ground begins to pile up on either side again and the beck enters a second and somewhat more forbidding ravine. Zig-zag up its rocky bed into the very heart of the gorge. When no further progress seems possible a steep groove on the right leads you on to easier ground.

If you find yourself deterred by this rocky finish retreat back down-gorge to find a grassy breach in its right wall. Either way, continue up steep grass and scree to join the path traversing below the summit crags of Harrison Stickle. Turn left along this to reach the grassy saddle between Loft Crag and Harrison Stickle and a junction with the 'tourist' route. Turn right now and a short climb brings you to the cairn of Harrison Stickle. The views are extensive, the highlights being Windermere to the south-east, the Scafells and Gable's rocky dome forming a rugged backcloth to the stony cone of neighbouring Pike o' Stickle, and close at hand the stark profile of Pavey Ark looming over dark Stickle Tarn.

Two interesting descents now present themselves. You may retrace your steps to the saddle and follow the 'tourist' route across the beck before bearing right to the cairn on Loft Crag. Now head north-westerly, along the edge of the escarpment, towards Pike o' Stickle. Shortly, look down to your left for a fine profile of Gimmer Crag, one of Lakeland's premier climbing grounds. Cross the head

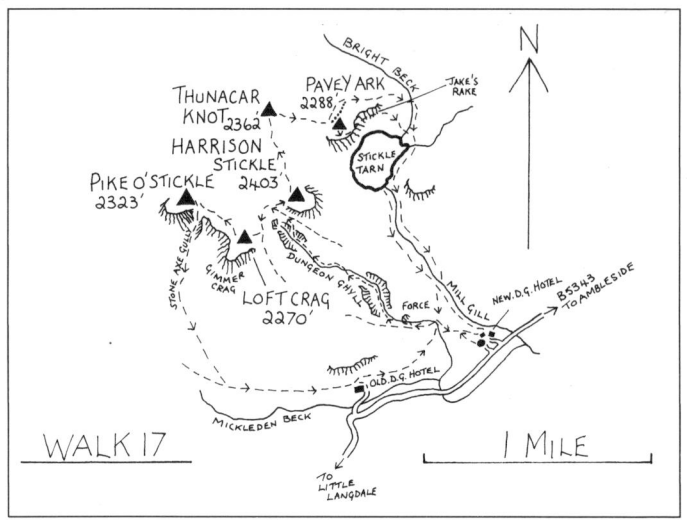

of Stone Axe Gully and scramble up to the cairn on Pike o' Stickle. Return to Langdale down Stone Axe Gully. (For descriptions of Pike o' Stickle and Stone Axe Gully refer to the end of Walk 18).

Alternatively, head north to bag the innocuous summit of Thunacar Knott, the site of another Neolithic stone axe factory. (See Walk 18). It is believed 'rough-out' axes were prepared in bulk at the mountain sites and then transported to the coastal settlements where New Red Sandstone and sand was available for polishing and grinding. The finished artifacts have been found in Ireland, Scotland and Southern England. Now head south-easterly to the cairn on Pavey Ark. Here, experienced scramblers may descend Jakes Rake to complete as good a day's scrambling as may be found in Lakeland. The inexperienced should leave Jakes Rake severely alone and follow the path running north-eastish, behind an old wall and the rim of the crag, then down a steep grassy corridor between rocks and on down to the bank of Bright Beck which is followed around to Stickle Tarn.

From the dam, built in 1824 to provide power for the Elterwater Gunpowder Company, follow a path on either bank of Mill Gill back to the New Dungeon Ghyll Hotel.

Walk 18   11 miles

A Great Langdale Horseshoe

THE Great Langdale Horseshoe, featured in that superbly produced book *The Big Walks*, starts and finishes at Elterwater and is eighteen miles long. Aesthetically and topographically this is the correct route and the walk described below is rather an Oxendale–Mickleden horseshoe. It is, however, the only Great Langdale Horseshoe I have so far done and is a splendid and quite strenuous walk in its own right covering the best and the most rugged sections of the longer walk.

Parking: As Walk 15.

RETURN to the main road, turn right then left and follow the road to eventually cross a cattle-grid close to a barn just past Wall End Farm. Beyond this the road steepens. Above the second hairpin a path will be seen bearing off to the right, above Redacre Gill. The ground steepens up a grassy tongue between two becks and a hard grind is endured before the head of the gill and easier ground is reached. From here you become aware just how much Bowfell dominates the Langdale Fells. Easy walking now leads to a steepening of the ground and some scrambling through the belt of rock guarding double-topped Pike o' Blisco. The slabby and highest point rises to the right across a rocky trench. From this cairn there is a detailed view of the rugged challenge facing you. Your eventual line of descent, Stone Axe Gully, is the pale slash scarring the craggy flank of Pike o' Stickle facing you across the depths of Oxendale and Mickleden.

Turn right, out of the rocky trench, and descend to the saddle above Red Tarn, a busy junction of fell paths. Climb up the far slope, slanting to the right of multiple-cairned Cold Pike — a short diversion left bags this peak. The angle eases before the rocky base of the first Crinkle, P2733 on the old 2½ inch map, is reached. From its stony summit the Isle of Man can be seen, given the right conditions, and the towers of Windscale peering threateningly over the foothills of Scafell. Crinkle is thought to be derived from the Old English 'cringol', meaning wrinkled or twisted. This rocky rollercoaster of summits, piled with slab and boulder, is unique in Lakeland and more reminiscent of many Scottish hills. Northwards, beyond a broad stony saddle rise the steep rocks of Long Top, at 2,816 feet the highest Crinkle. They are split by a wide gully crowned with a huge jammed block. Many walkers appear to be deterred by this and traverse left along the base of the rocks to easier ground — they miss all the fun! A heave and and a couple of quick steps up the right-hand wall and it's all over. A scramble up and around the head of the gully brings a short easy walk to the summit cairn. The royal Scafells, split by the savage breach of Mickledore — the Great Door, now command the north-western skyline.

The topography of Crinkle Crags is complicated — Long Top cairn lies at right angles to the main ridge. A heading north, however, will suffice to bring you safely down to the Three Tarns saddle. The rumour that compasses are jinxed on Crinkle Crags and Bowfell is untrue as long as you don't stand them on a rock to take your bearing. The path is well-worn and in good weather the way is obvious — a succession of rocky tors, grassy saddles and some delightful pools, with Bowfell challenging ahead and superb all-round views. The main 'trod' takes the easiest line, wending rather than topping, which is a pity because that is what it's all about. It completely by-passes the fine tor of clean rock which is the summit of Shelter Crags, a two-thousand footer in its own right!

From the Three Tarns saddle escape can be made, if desired, by turning right and down to Langdale by way of The Band. The way to Bowfell is obvious, a badly eroded path climbing steeply up between a file of gullies to the left, Bowfell Links, and a rib of broken slabby rocks. This rib gives a pleasant scrambly alternative to the trod. Either brings you out onto a broad rocky ridge with the cone of piled boulders that forms the summit of Bowfell rising to your left. Given a fine day don't immediately bear left but head across the ridge to reach and stand upon the upper rim of The Great Slab, featured on the front cover of Wainwright's *Fellwanderer*. Below, to the left, rise the slanting columnar rocks of Bowfell Buttress, a popular climbing crag. Now head for Bowfell summit.

Just west of and below the spiky summit rocks two leaning boulders form a squashy cave for two. My wife Joyce and I were wedged into this one day trying to open a tin of tuna with a rock, having forgotten the tin opener. We uncorked ourselves hurriedly when every seagull in the Western Approaches began strafing the tuna-bespattered summit of Bowfell.

From Bowfell top follow the cairns northwards and down to pass above a steep scree gully dividing Cambridge Crag and Bowfell Buttress. This often gives a straightforward but entertaining snow climb, being invariably crowned with a handsome cornice. Near here the worn path now veers left onto the western flank of the fell. Ignore this and continue northwards along the broad stony undulating ridge to the farthest cairn. This is unnamed on the map, listed as 'Bowfell North' by George Bridge in his *Mountains of England and Wales',* the English peak-baggers' bible, and popularly as Hanging Knotts. Go beyond this cairn to find a faint path bearing right and down into a rocky hollow which often retains a patch of snow into early summer. Now bear left down bouldery terraces followed by steep grass to reach the crest of Rossett Gill — which offers another escape route to Langdale, if desired.

Now climb the ridge curving easterly to capture the summit of Rossett Pike. Go beyond the summit cairn to find a path bearing left, north-easterly, which slants down across the south-east face of the fell, passing below a grassy saddle, to reach a wide grassy shelf below a crag, Black Crag. Beyond the shelf turn right and down to join the Stake Pass path. A further escape could be made here by turning right, down to Mickleden. From here, the last summit of your horseshoe, Pike o' Stickle, thrusts its stony cone over the next rise.

To continue, follow the Stake Pass path across the beck then turn almost immediately right to climb a fainter path to reach the cairn on Mart Crag. The angle eases now and the ground becomes boggier before it steepens again and the path bears right to reach the base of the Pike o' Stickle summit rocks. A short scramble reaches the cairn from where you can look back with justifiable pride at the rugged and serrated skyline you have traversed. A nineteenth-century fellwalker wrote of Pike o' Stickle, 'The view down Langdale is enough to make a person of good nerves tremble, though the top of the Pike is not so sharp a point as it seems from a distance.'

Now descend to the head of the wide gully beyond, Stone Axe Gully. Decades of slithering boots have played havoc with its shifting surface but its descent presents no problem as long as care is taken. The rock architecture on either side is superb. It is the reputedly man-made square-cut cave in its western wall, several hundred feet down, which is the main attraction, however. Here a chance discovery in 1947 revealed the first of Lakeland's stone axe factories. Subsequently, other sites have been found on the Langdale Pikes, Glaramara and Scafell Pike. Practical experiments using teams of men clearing forest with axes of the Pike o' Stickle type appear to prove that it was Neolithic man who first began to shape the Lakeland landscape we see today. A final stony glissade reaches the turfy flats of Mickleden and an easy plod back to the start.

The alternative descent to Stone Axe Gully, perhaps easier but longer, is to follow the ridge south-easterly to the summit of Loft

Crag and from there bear left to join and follow the well-worn path that leads back down to Langdale.

Walk 19 — 9 miles

Bowfell, via Hell Gill and the Climbers' Traverse

THE rugged Oxendale flank of Crinkle Crags is cleaved by four gills, reading from right to left, Hell Gill, Crinkle Gill, Isaac Gill and Brown Gill. Hell, Crinkle and Brown Gills offer a triumvirate of splendid scrambles. Hell Gill, however, slants away towards Bowfell and, combined with the Climbers' Traverse, gives a flavour of real mountaineering to an ascent of this fine fell.

Parking: As Walk 15.

WALK back to the main road, turn right and, passing through the gate ahead, follow the unfenced track to Stool End Farm. Behind the farm rises the broad ridge known as The Band. Ignore all paths save that following the wall leading into the valley to the left of The Band. This is Oxendale, a lovely spot to spend a leisurely hot afternoon with its clear pools and green turf.

Eventually a footbridge is reached at a confluence of gills. If you cross the bridge and turn right a path takes you above Whorneyside Force and on to the entrance of Hell Gill. A more interesting way, however, giving a far finer view of this splendid waterfall, is to turn right just before the bridge and scramble along the right bank of the gill to reach the pool at its foot. Scramble to the top of the fall by grassy ledges to its right and follow the beck above to the narrow entrance of Hell Gill. In a dry summer, if you have a steady head, it would probably be possible to climb up the slabby rocks flanking the cascade. The little pool above the fall gives a very refreshing dip on a hot day.

The entrance to Hell Gill has something of an 'all hope abandon, ye who enter here' look about it. It is narrow, high-walled, moated by an icy pool, and in spate would doubtless be impossible. After some enjoyable and torturous scrambling the gill widens, although the walls on either side remain impressively steep and high. Beyond

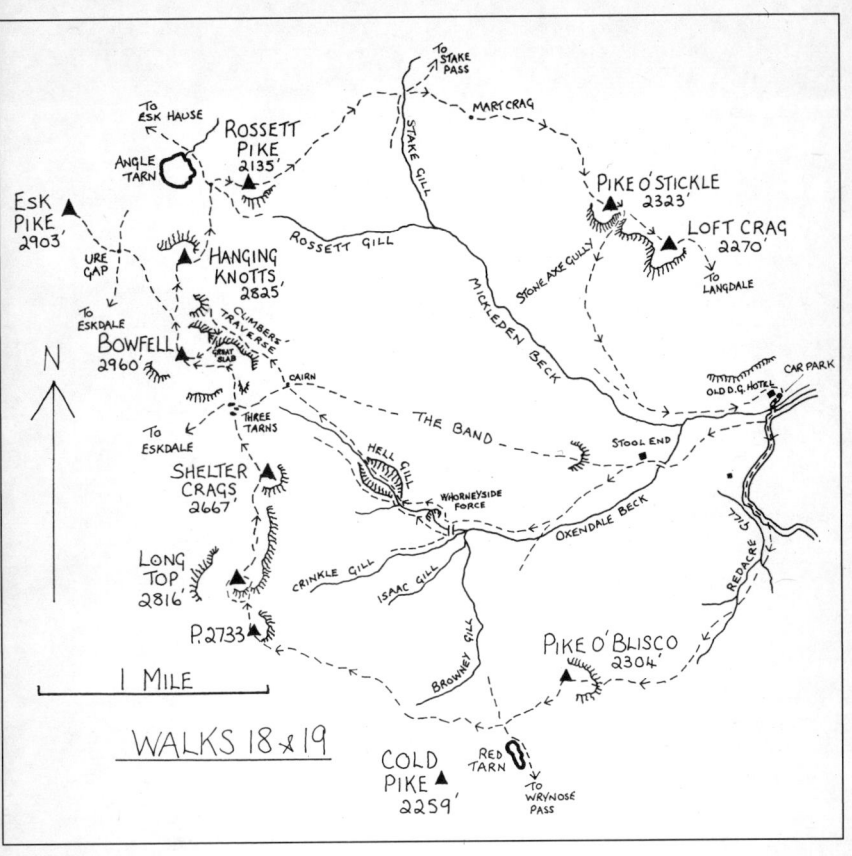

this the gill forks. So far the appearance of both forks has deterred us from attempting them without a rope, and we have escaped up airy grassy ledges on the dividing buttress. For anyone deterred by the gill entrance, or extreme conditions, a path climbs along the rim of the left wall giving airy views down into the depths.

Above, Hell Gill is just another innocuous mountain beck curving up to its source close under the saddle of Three Tarns. Continue along the right bank of the beck, aiming for the skyline ahead. On the right the head of The Band ridge sweeps up in tiers of broken rock towards the hidden summit of Bowfell. Across the foot of these rocks slants Bowfell's well worn 'tourist route' via The Band. You head for the skyline and the lowest point of the rocks, crossing the 'tourist route'.

Once on the crest, look for a cairn indicating the point where a narrow path debouches onto the far flank of the ridge. This is the start of the 'Climbers' Traverse'. This delightful path twists and slants across a steep rough fellside to reach and pass below the base of the compact overhanging walls of Flat Crags. The 'traverse' continues beyond Flat Crags to the foot of Cambridge Crag, then across a broad scree gully to the foot of the slanting columnar rocks of Bowfell Buttress. This gully gives a splendid but straightforward snow climb in the right conditions, usually and excitingly being topped by a handsome cornice. Bowfell Buttress was named after the climb running centrally up its tilted rocks. First climbed by T. Shaw in 1902, it still remains one of Lakeland's great 'classic' rock climbs.

You leave the 'traverse' beyond Flat Crags to follow a path climbing up a bouldery chute between the latter crag and Cambridge Crag. (If you are thirsty there is a spring of pure chilled water seeping out of the rocks at the foot of Cambridge Crag). The slanting roof of Flat Crags forms the Great Slab which figures on the jacket of Wainwright's *Fellwanderer*. If the rock is dry move away from the bouldery path and walk up this easy-angled slab. When the crest of the ridge is reached turn right to shortly reach the boulder-piled summit of Bowfell, and a magnificent view of the Scafells cleaved by the savage gash of Mickledore.

From Bowfell top head north, passing across the crest of the scree gully dividing Bowfell Buttress from Cambridge Crag, to reach the cairn on Hanging Knott. Beyond this bear right down into a rocky hollow, which often retains a patch of snow into early summer, then left down bouldery terraces followed by steep grass to the crest of Rossett Gill. To avoid Rossett Gill's renowned knee-jellying ordeal, climb the ridge curving easterly to the summit of Rossett Pike.

Rossett Pike is an attractive little peak, all too often by-passed. From the foot of Rossett Gill it forms an almost perfect pyramid. Go beyond its summit cairn to find a path bearing left which slants across the south-east face of the fell, passing below a col and across an obvious grassy shelf beneath Black Crag, to a junction with Stake Gill and the Stake Pass path. It gives an unusual prospect of ice-scooped Mickleden and the 'wrong' side of the Langdale Pikes.

Turn down the zig-zags to Mickleden and follow its turfy flats back to journey's end.